COOK'S COLLECTION

LIGHT & HEALTHY

Fuss-free and tasty recipe ideas
for the modern cook

CONTENTS

INTRODUCTION

Healthy eating shouldn't be about sticking to a strict diet or banning foods you love from your daily menu. It's about celebrating feeling good, having a positive attitude towards food, maintaining a healthy weight and having more energy as you go through the day. Combining a good diet with regular exercise will keep you healthy right through your life.

These days, deciding what you should be eating can be a bit confusing, with a new expert opinion or fad diet popping up every other day, but the key to healthy eating is balance. Science still hasn't identified all the nutrients in every food, so eating a broad range of ingredients from all the major food groups is a good way to ensure that you're getting a balanced diet that will promote good health and help you fight illness and disease. And trying new ingredients is fun – no one wants to eat the same meal every day all in the name of healthy eating!

One of the best ways to make your diet as healthy as possible is to cook from scratch with fresh ingredients –

however tempting ready-made sauces, soups, dressings and gravies, and the deliciously inventive ranges of supermarket ready meals are, they are usually loaded with salt, sugar and chemical additives. And if you can't pronounce an ingredient, it suddenly becomes less appealing! If you cook your own meals with fresh ingredients, you'll be surprised at how little salt and sugar you'll need to add and you'll be safe in the knowledge that you know exactly what's gone into a dish.

Be sure to include lots of fruit, vegetables and pulses in your diet too – it's no coincidence that almost all of the nutrient-dense foods that are labelled superfoods, from avocados to blueberries to lentils to sweet potatoes, are plant-based. Natural, plant-based meals are an easy way to eat a rainbow of ingredients, and it's fun to mix up your week by eating vegetarian. Even breakfast can include a healthy dose of fruit and vegetables.

Have a couple of meat-free days every week so that your digestive system can take a breather – it will also give you the chance to discover just how delicious and versatile vegetables and pulses can be. Even if you're a confirmed carnivore, you should eat at least five portions of fruit and veg every day – tip the balance in favour of vegetables, as most fruits have a high sugar content.

Don't fear fat – good fat, that is! Fats are an essential part of a healthy diet, but you should be getting them from nuts, seeds, vegetables and oily fish, which supply plenty of those all-important omega-3 fats. Try to keep your intake of saturated fats (the bad fat) from butter, cheese and meat to a minimum. Trans fats (often listed as hydrogenated fats) are much worse than saturated fats and often pop up in those handy ready-made ingredients such as pastry, and in ready-made cookies, cakes and pies, so always read the label carefully. Replace butter or oil with coconut oil when cooking – don't worry, the aroma of coconut disappears!

Eat plenty of whole grains – a breakfast of porridge or granola is a great start to your day. Swap refined pasta and rice for wholegrain varieties – they are far more nutritious and provide plenty of that essential dietary fibre. Always go for wholegrain breads with nuts and seeds added instead of white. Try breads made with buckwheat (which is a seed, rather than a grain) and spelt (an ancient grain with a low gluten content), and make delicious meal-in-a-bowl salads with high-protein farro or quinoa and those tiny but nutritionally dense chia seeds.

Watch what you drink – alcohol and soft drinks are high in sugar and calories, so enjoy them in moderation or, even better, swap them for sparkling water. Drink plenty of water to prevent tiredness, dehydration and headaches. If you find still water too unexciting, mix some sparkling water with a little fruit juice, or try experimenting with herbal teas and infused waters – there are tons of great flavour combinations out there. Try substituting cow's milk for unsweetened almond, rice or oat milk.

Sugar has become public enemy number one in recent years and it's best to avoid a high consumption. Even if you think your diet is low in sugar, you might be surprised by how many products contain a hefty serving, including soups and savoury ready meals. You can indulge a sweet tooth with some of the great natural sugar substitutes that are available. Sweeten cakes and cookies with bananas or apples, or with raisins, dried figs or dates, a dash of manuka honey or agave syrup or a little stevia. The sweet treats in this book tweak the sugar load of your favourite desserts and cakes – try Chocolate & Chia Puddings (see page 158). Who knew sweet could be good for you!

Snacking doesn't have to be unhealthy. For a quick boost, reach for some energy-packed nuts or seeds or a piece of fruit rather than a chocolate bar or bag of crisps. Or, if you have a little time, make some of the healthy snacks included in this book like Chicken, Kale & Chia Seed Bites (see page 74) or some Apple & Cinnamon Crisps (see page 73).

And most importantly, enjoy your food! A little indulgence every now and then shouldn't fill you with guilt. The delicious and wholesome recipes in this book will give you all the inspiration you need to start eating well and feeling good.

CHAPTER ONE

BREAKFAST

COCONUT
POWER BOWL

SERVES: *4* | **PREP:** *20 mins* | **COOK:** *15 mins*

INGREDIENTS

100 g/3½ oz coconut oil
1 tbsp honey
2 tbsp dark muscovado sugar
100 g/3½ oz quinoa flakes
150 g/5½ oz rolled oats
3 tbsp desiccated coconut
½ tsp ground cinnamon
1 tbsp dried cranberries
1 tbsp chopped pecan nuts
2 bananas, peeled and chopped
55 g/2 oz walnuts
200 ml/7 fl oz coconut milk
1 tsp ground cinnamon
100 g/3½ oz raspberries
small handful of mint leaves
2 tbsp maple syrup

1. Preheat the oven to 180°C/350°F/Gas Mark 4. Put the coconut oil, honey and sugar into a saucepan over a low heat and heat, stirring, until the sugar has dissolved.

2. Remove from the heat and stir in the quinoa flakes, 55 g/2 oz of the oats, 2 tablespoons of the desiccated coconut, the cinnamon, cranberries and pecan nuts. Mix well to combine.

3. Spread the mixture over a baking sheet and bake in the preheated oven for 15 minutes, stirring halfway through the cooking time.

4. Remove the granola from the oven, spoon into a bowl and leave to cool.

5. Meanwhile, place the bananas, the remaining oats, the walnuts and coconut milk in a food processor and process until the mixture is almost smooth.

6. Pour into four bowls and add the granola. Top with the cinnamon, raspberries, mint, the remaining desiccated coconut and a drizzle of maple syrup.

MILLET PORRIDGE
WITH APRICOT PURÉE

INGREDIENTS

225 g/8 oz millet flakes
450 ml/16 fl oz soya milk
pinch of salt

APRICOT PURÉE

115 g/4 oz dried apricots, roughly
*   chopped*
300 ml/10 fl oz water

1. To make the apricot purée, put the apricots into a saucepan and cover with the water. Bring to the boil, then reduce the heat and simmer, half covered, for 20 minutes until the apricots are very tender. Use a hand-held blender or transfer the apricots, along with any water left in the pan, to a food processor or blender and process until smooth. Set aside.

2. To make the porridge, put the millet flakes into a clean saucepan and add the milk and salt. Bring to the boil, then reduce the heat and simmer for 5 minutes, stirring frequently, until cooked and creamy.

3. To serve, spoon into four bowls and top with the apricot purée.

CHIA SEED & PISTACHIO BREAKFAST PUDDING

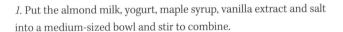
SERVES: *4* | **PREP:** *5 mins, plus chilling* | **COOK:** *No cooking*

INGREDIENTS

*225 ml/8 fl oz unsweetened almond
 milk*

*225 ml/8 fl oz low-fat natural
 yogurt*

2 tbsp pure maple syrup

1½ tsp vanilla extract

pinch of salt

35 g/1¼ oz chia seeds

225 g/8 oz strawberries, sliced

*40 g/1½ oz toasted pistachio nuts,
 chopped*

maple syrup, for drizzling (optional)

1. Put the almond milk, yogurt, maple syrup, vanilla extract and salt into a medium-sized bowl and stir to combine.

2. Stir in the chia seeds and leave to stand for about 30 minutes at room temperature. Stir the mixture well to make sure the seeds are well incorporated, then cover and chill in the refrigerator for at least 8 hours or overnight.

3. To serve, spoon the pudding into serving bowls and top with the strawberries, nuts and a drizzle of maple syrup, if using.

CITRUS FRUIT REFRESHER

SERVES: *4* | **PREP:** *20 mins* | **COOK:** *No cooking*

INGREDIENTS

1 ruby grapefruit

1 pink grapefruit

2 oranges

1 honeydew melon, halved,
  deseeded, peeled and cut
  into chunks

finely grated zest and juice of 1 lime

25 g/1 oz fresh mint, finely
  shredded

2 tbsp clear honey

1. Cut the peel and pith away from the ruby grapefruit, pink grapefruit and the oranges with a small serrated knife. Hold one of the fruits above a bowl and cut between the membranes to release the segments. Squeeze the juice from the membranes into the bowl. Continue until all the fruits have been segmented into the bowl.

2. Add the melon, lime zest and juice and half the mint. Drizzle over the honey, then gently stir with a large spoon. Decorate with the remaining mint and serve.

FRUITY
GRANOLA CUPS

SERVES: *2* | **PREP:** *25 mins* | **COOK:** *35 mins*

INGREDIENTS

115 g/4 oz medium oatmeal

85 g/3 oz porridge oats

*40 g/1½ oz unblanched almonds,
    roughly chopped*

2 tbsp pumpkin seeds

2 tbsp sunflower seeds

2 tbsp milled linseeds

½ tsp ground cinnamon

3 tbsp maple syrup

1 tbsp olive oil

25 g/1 oz goji berries

TO SERVE

115 g/4 oz granola

juice of 1 orange

*115 g/4 oz Greek-style natural
    yogurt*

*1 dessert apple, cored and coarsely
    grated*

*115 g/4 oz strawberries, hulled and
    sliced*

40 g/1½ oz blueberries

1. Preheat the oven to 160°C/325°F/Gas Mark 3. Put the oatmeal, oats and almonds in a bowl. Stir in the pumpkin seeds, sunflower seeds and linseeds, then add the cinnamon, maple syrup and oil and stir to combine.

2. Tip the granola into a roasting tin, then spread in an even layer. Bake in the preheated oven for 30–35 minutes, or until golden brown all over, stirring every 5–10 minutes and mixing any browner granola from the edges of the tin into the centre after 15 minutes.

3. Stir in the goji berries, then leave to cool. Pack into an airtight container and store in the refrigerator for up to five days.

4. When ready to serve, spoon the granola into two glasses or bowls, reserving a little for the top. Moisten with the orange juice. Mix the yogurt with the apple, spoon over the granola, top with the strawberries and blueberries and sprinkle with the reserved granola.

HEALTHY FRENCH TOAST

SERVES: *4* | **PREP:** *20 mins* | **COOK:** *12–17 mins*

INGREDIENTS

60 g/2¼ oz pecan nuts, roughly
  chopped
2 eggs
4 ripe bananas, sliced
½ tsp vanilla extract
½ tsp ground cinnamon
4 thick slices wholemeal bread
1 tbsp olive oil
½ tsp ground cinnamon,
  for sprinkling

1. Place the pecan nuts in a small, dry frying pan and toast over a medium heat for 3–4 minutes, tossing regularly until just toasted. Set aside until needed.

2. Place the eggs, 2 bananas, the vanilla extract and cinnamon in a blender and whizz for 1–2 minutes, or until the consistency is smooth and thick.

3. Pour the mixture into a medium-sized shallow dish. Place two slices of bread in the mixture and, working quickly, gently press the bread into the liquid, allowing it to soak up the mixture. Turn the slices over and repeat.

4. Meanwhile, heat half the oil in a large, non-stick frying pan over a medium–high heat. Using a spatula, remove the soaked bread from the banana mixture and place in the pan. Cook for 2–3 minutes on each side, then remove from the pan, set aside and keep warm. Repeat the process for the remaining slices, adding the remaining oil if needed.

5. Serve the banana bread immediately, with a sprinkling of cinnamon and the pecan nuts and remaining sliced bananas on top.

BUCKWHEAT PANCAKES
WITH RASPBERRY SAUCE

SERVES: *4* | **PREP:** *5 mins, plus resting and cooling* | **COOK:** *15 mins*

INGREDIENTS

1 egg

275 ml/9 fl oz skimmed milk

½ tsp salt

2 tsp sunflower oil

60 g/2¼ oz wholemeal flour

60 g/2¼ oz buckwheat flour

cooking oil spray, for frying

RASPBERRY SAUCE

250 g/9 oz raspberries

2 tbsp water

2 tbsp stevia granules

1. Beat the egg in a mixing bowl, then stir in the milk, salt and oil and beat until well combined. Put the wholemeal flour and buckwheat flour into a separate bowl and mix together. Stir the milk mixture into the flour mixture and beat until smooth. Cover and leave to rest for up to 30 minutes.

2. Meanwhile, to make the raspberry sauce, gently heat the raspberries with the water in a saucepan until the juices run. Stir in the stevia until the granules are completely dissolved. Push through a fine sieve to remove any pips. Leave to cool completely.

3. When ready to make the pancakes, place a small frying pan over a high heat and add 4 sprays of cooking oil. When the oil is very hot, spoon one eighth of the batter into the pan and swirl around to coat the base of the pan evenly. Cook for 1–2 minutes until the underside of the pancake is nicely golden. Turn the pancake over with a large spatula and cook until golden on the other side. Remove and keep the pancake warm while you cook the remaining pancakes, spraying the pan each time with up to 4 sprays of oil, or as necessary.

4. Serve the pancakes on four warmed plates and pour over the raspberry sauce.

BREAKFAST
POWER BALLS

SERVES: *4* | **PREP:** *15 mins, plus chilling* | **COOK:** *No cooking*

INGREDIENTS

70 g/2½ oz ground almonds

70 g/2½ oz cashew nuts, finely chopped

3 tbsp milled linseeds

40 g/1½ oz raw cacao

100 g/3½ oz ready-to-eat dried apricots, finely chopped

1 tbsp maple syrup

½ tsp vanilla extract

1 large ripe dessert pear, cored and cut into thin slices

2 oranges, cut into segments

1. Place the almonds, half the cashew nuts, the linseeds, cacao, apricots, maple syrup and vanilla extract in a mixing bowl. Mix thoroughly until well combined – add a few drops of cold water if the mixture does not come together easily. Divide the mixture into 16 pieces and roll each piece into a ball.

2. Put the remaining cashew nuts into a shallow bowl. Dip each ball into the nuts and turn until lightly coated. Transfer to an airtight container and refrigerate for several hours before eating.

3. To serve, arrange the pear slices and orange segments on four serving plates. Place four balls on each plate and serve immediately.

BREAKFAST
BERRY SMOOTHIE

SERVES: *2* | **PREP:** *10 mins* | **COOK:** *No cooking*

INGREDIENTS

200 g/7 oz strawberries
100 g/3½ oz raspberries
150 ml/5 fl oz milk
40 g/1½ oz unsweetened muesli

1. Reserve one strawberry for decoration and cut in half.

2. Remove the hulls from the remaining strawberries. Place the strawberries, raspberries, milk and unsweetened muesli in a food processor or blender.

3. Process until almost smooth.

4. Pour into glasses, top each smoothie with half a strawberry and serve immediately.

MUESLI
MOTIVATOR JUICE

INGREDIENTS

20 g/¾ oz porridge oats
25 g/1 oz flaked almonds
½ ruby red grapefruit, zest and a
  little pith removed
150 g/5½ oz raspberries
juice of 2 oranges
125 ml/4 fl oz chilled water

1. Put the porridge oats and almonds in a blender and whizz until finely ground.

2. Deseed and roughly chop the grapefruit. Be sure to cut the grapefruit into small pieces before putting it in your blender so that you get a smooth juice.

3. Add the grapefruit, raspberries, orange juice and water and whizz until smooth.

4. Pour into a glass and serve immediately.

BERRY
WHIP SMOOTHIE

SERVES: *4* | **PREP:** *10–15 mins* | **COOK:** *No cooking*

INGREDIENTS

125 g/4½ oz frozen sliced
   strawberries
125 g/4½ oz frozen blueberries
40 g/1½ oz Brazil nuts, chopped
40 g/1½ oz cashew nut pieces
25 g/1 oz porridge oats
450 ml/16 fl oz almond milk
2 tbsp maple syrup

1. Place the strawberries, blueberries, Brazil nuts and cashew nut pieces in a blender. Sprinkle over the oats, then pour in half the almond milk. Blend until smooth.

2. Add the remaining milk and the maple syrup, and blend again until smooth.

3. Pour into four glasses and serve immediately with spoons. As the drink stands, the blueberries will almost set the liquid, but as soon as you stir it, it will become liquid again.

JUMBO CARROT CAKE BISCUITS

MAKES: *12 biscuits* | **PREP:** *30 mins* | **COOK:** *20 mins*

INGREDIENTS

100 g/3½ oz linseeds
85 g/3 oz plain wholemeal flour
70 g/2½ oz porridge oats
1 tsp baking powder
1 tsp ground ginger
2 tsp ground cinnamon
85 g/3 oz dried apricots, finely
*   chopped*
1 dessert apple, cored and coarsely
*   grated*
1 carrot, finely grated
40 g/1½ oz pecan nuts
3 tbsp coconut oil
125 ml/4 fl oz maple syrup
grated zest of ½ orange, plus 3 tbsp
*   juice*
4 tbsp dried coconut shavings

1. Preheat the oven to 180°C/350°F/Gas Mark 4 and line two baking sheets with baking paper.

2. Put the linseeds in a blender and process to a fine powder, then tip into a mixing bowl. Add the flour, oats and baking powder, then the ginger and cinnamon, and stir well. Add the apricots, apple and carrot. Roughly chop the pecan nuts and stir into the mixture.

3. Warm the coconut oil in a small saucepan (or in the microwave for 30 seconds) until just liquid. Remove from the heat, then stir in the maple syrup and orange zest and juice. Pour this into the carrot mixture and stir together until you have a soft dough.

4. Spoon 12 mounds of the mixture onto the prepared baking sheets, then flatten them into thick 7.5-cm/3-inch diameter rounds. Sprinkle with the coconut shavings, then bake in the preheated oven for 15–18 minutes, or until brown.

5. Serve warm or leave to cool, then pack into a plastic container and store in the refrigerator for up to 3 days.

ASPARAGUS WITH HOT-SMOKED SALMON

INGREDIENTS

50 g/1¾ oz unsalted butter,
softened
finely grated zest of ½ unwaxed
lemon, plus ½ tsp juice
sprig of fresh dill, roughly chopped
400 g/14 oz hot-smoked salmon
1 tsp salt
10 asparagus spears, woody stalks
removed
2 large eggs
sea salt and pepper (optional)

1. Preheat the oven to 180°C/350°F/Gas Mark 4. Put the butter, lemon zest and juice and dill in a small bowl, season to taste with salt and pepper, if using, and mix. Pat the butter into a rough square with the back of a spoon, wrap it in clingfilm and chill in the refrigerator while you prepare the rest of the dish.

2. Wrap the salmon in foil and bake in the preheated oven for 15 minutes. Flake the fish into bite-sized pieces and keep warm.

3. Add the salt to a large saucepan of water and bring to the boil, then add the asparagus, bring back to the boil and cook for 2 minutes. Drain and rinse briefly under cold running water to stop the cooking process, then set aside.

4. Bring a shallow saucepan of water to a gentle simmer. Crack an egg into a small bowl, then slide the egg into the water, lowering the bowl as close to the water as possible. Using a large spoon, gently fold any stray strands of white around the yolk. Cook for 3½–4 minutes, then remove with a slotted spoon. Repeat with the remaining egg.

5. Divide the asparagus spears between two plates, top with half the salmon, then place a poached egg on top and crown with a dab of the lemon butter. Serve immediately.

BUBBLE & SQUEAK
BREAKFAST BOWL

SERVES: *2* | **PREP:** *5 mins* | **COOK:** *10 mins*

INGREDIENTS

400 g/14 oz sweet potato, peeled
*   and cut into chunks*
200 g/7 oz kale, chopped
2 eggs
2 tsp coconut oil
1 tsp cumin seeds
1 tsp mustard seeds
1 tsp pepper
½ tsp ground turmeric
25 g/1 oz walnuts, chopped
25 g/1 oz blanched almonds,
*   chopped*
25 g/1 oz pumpkin seeds

1. Place the sweet potato in a steamer and cook for 5–6 minutes until tender. Add the kale to the steamer for the last 2 minutes of cooking.

2. Bring a shallow saucepan of water to a gentle simmer. Crack an egg into a small bowl, then slide the egg into the water, lowering the bowl as close to the water as possible. Using a large spoon, gently fold any stray strands of white around the yolk. Poach for 3½–4 minutes, then repeat with the remaining egg.

3. Heat the oil in a large frying pan or wok and add the cumin seeds, mustard seeds, pepper and turmeric. Cook until the mustard seeds begin to 'pop', then add the steamed vegetables and toss.

4. Divide the spiced vegetables between two warmed bowls and top each one with a poached egg.

5. Sprinkle each serving with walnuts, almonds and pumpkin seeds and serve immediately.

EGG-WHITE OMELETTE
WITH SPICY THREE-BEAN FILLING

SERVES: *1* | **PREP:** *10 mins* | **COOK:** *10 mins*

INGREDIENTS

4 egg whites

¼ tsp salt

1 tbsp water

2 tsp oil from a jar of
*   semi-dried tomatoes*

2 spring onions, finely chopped

85 g/3 oz cooked mixed beans,
*   rinsed*

40 g/1½ oz frozen sweetcorn,
*   thawed*

50 ml/2 fl oz hot tomato salsa

3 semi-dried tomatoes in oil,
*   drained and chopped*

½ tsp smoked paprika

2 tbsp chopped fresh coriander

5 sprays cooking oil spray

1. Put the egg whites into a bowl with the salt and water and beat well together.

2. Place the oil in a small frying pan over a medium heat. Add the spring onion and fry for 1 minute until soft.

3. Add the beans and sweetcorn to the pan with the tomato salsa, tomatoes and paprika. Cook for a few minutes, then stir in half of the coriander. Set the mixture aside and keep warm.

4. Spray a separate small frying pan with the cooking oil spray and heat over a high heat until very hot. Pour in the egg white mixture and cook, making sure that the egg cooks evenly. When the underside of the omelette is golden and the top is cooked but still moist, spoon the bean filling over the top, then sprinkle over the remaining coriander.

5. Tip the pan gently to one side, fold the omelette in half and slide onto a warmed serving plate. Serve immediately.

POACHED EGGS & KALE WITH SOURDOUGH

SERVES: *4* | **PREP:** *20 mins* | **COOK:** *15–17 mins*

INGREDIENTS

4 eggs
100 g/3½ oz kale, chopped
4 large slices wholemeal
    sourdough bread
2 garlic cloves, halved
2 tbsp olive oil
1 tsp dried red chilli flakes

1. Bring a shallow saucepan of water to a gentle simmer. Crack an egg into a small bowl, then slide the egg into the water, lowering the bowl as close to the water as possible. Using a large spoon, gently fold any stray strands of white around the yolk. Repeat with the remaining eggs.

2. Cook the eggs for 3½–4 minutes, or until set to your liking, then remove with a slotted spoon. Place the eggs in a small bowl of warm water and set aside.

3. Bring a saucepan of water to the boil and add the kale. Simmer for 3–4 minutes, or until the kale is just cooked but still retains a little crunch. Drain and set aside.

4. Meanwhile, toast the bread. Place the toast on four plates, then rub with garlic and drizzle with the oil. Top each slice with some blanched kale and a poached egg. Finally, sprinkle over chilli flakes. Serve immediately.

BAKED MUSHROOMS
WITH HERB RICOTTA

SERVES: *4* | **PREP:** *10 mins* | **COOK:** *15–20 mins*

INGREDIENTS

4 large flat mushrooms
1 tbsp olive oil
1 shallot, roughly chopped
25 g/1 oz fresh flat-leaf parsley
1 tbsp snipped fresh chives
140 g/5 oz ricotta cheese
salt and pepper (optional)

1. Preheat the oven to 200°C/400°F/Gas Mark 6. Remove the stalks from the mushrooms and set aside. Place the mushrooms in a shallow baking dish and brush with the oil.

2. Put the mushroom stalks, shallot, parsley and chives in a food processor and blend until finely chopped. Season to taste with salt and pepper, if using.

3. Place the chopped ingredients in a large bowl with the ricotta cheese and stir to mix evenly.

4. Spoon the herb ricotta on top of the mushrooms. Bake in the preheated oven for 15–20 minutes, or until tender and bubbling. Serve immediately.

COURGETTE FRITTERS

INGREDIENTS

85 g/3 oz brown rice flour

1 tsp baking powder

2 eggs, beaten

200 ml/7 fl oz milk

250 g/9 oz courgettes

2 tbsp fresh thyme leaves

1 tbsp virgin olive oil

salt and pepper (optional)

1. Sift the flour and baking powder into a large bowl, then tip the remaining bran in the sieve into the bowl. Make a well in the centre. Pour the eggs into the well and, using a wooden spoon, gradually draw in the flour. Slowly pour in the milk, stirring constantly to form a thick batter.

2. Meanwhile, place kitchen paper on a plate and grate the courgettes over it so it absorbs some of the juices. Pat the courgettes dry, then add them to the batter with the thyme, season with salt and pepper, if using, and mix well.

3. Heat the oil in a frying pan over a medium–high heat. Drop tablespoons of the batter into the pan, leaving a little space between them. Cook in batches for 3–4 minutes on each side, or until the fritters are golden brown.

4. Line a baking sheet with kitchen paper. Transfer the fritters to the baking sheet using a slotted spoon and leave to drain well. Remove the kitchen paper and keep each batch warm while you make the rest. Allow five fritters per person and serve immediately.

SHAKSHUKA EGGS WITH SPICY TOMATO SAUCE

SERVES: 4 | **PREP:** 10 mins | **COOK:** 35 mins

INGREDIENTS

1 tsp cumin seeds

1 tsp coriander seeds

2 tsp olive oil

1 onion, finely chopped

600 g/1 lb 5 oz canned plum
    tomatoes

40 g/1½ oz chilli pesto

¼ tsp saffron

¼ tsp cayenne pepper

½ tsp salt

1 tsp pepper

3 tbsp chopped fresh coriander

4 large eggs

1. Crush the cumin seeds and coriander seeds. Place a non-stick frying pan over a medium heat and add the seeds to the pan. Stir for 1 minute, or until their aromas are released.

2. Reduce the heat to medium–low, add the oil and heat. Add the onion and cook, stirring occasionally, for 5 minutes, or until the onion is soft and just turning slightly golden.

3. Add the tomatoes, breaking up any large ones, pesto, saffron, cayenne pepper, salt and pepper. Stir well, bring to a simmer and cook for 15 minutes, adding a little hot water towards the end if the pan looks too dry (but you don't want the sauce to be too runny). Stir in half the fresh coriander.

4. Make four wells in the sauce and break an egg into each one. Cover the pan and cook over a low heat for 10 minutes, or until the egg whites are set but the yolks are still runny. Sprinkle the remaining fresh coriander over the top and serve immediately.

HEALTHY BREAKFAST FRITTATA

SERVES: *4* | **PREP:** *15 mins* | **COOK:** *20 mins*

INGREDIENTS

250 g/9 oz baby new potatoes,
   unpeeled and sliced
2 tbsp virgin olive oil
4 spring onions, thinly sliced
1 courgette, thinly sliced
115 g/4 oz baby spinach, de-stalked
¼ tsp smoked hot paprika
6 eggs
salt and pepper (optional)

1. Bring a saucepan of water to the boil, add the potatoes and cook for 5 minutes, or until just tender, then drain well.

2. Meanwhile, heat 1 tablespoon of the oil in a large ovenproof frying pan over a medium heat. Add the spring onions, courgette and potatoes and fry, stirring and turning the vegetables, for 5 minutes, or until just beginning to brown.

3. Add the spinach and paprika and cook, stirring, for 1–2 minutes, or until the spinach leaves have just wilted.

4. Preheat the grill to medium–hot. Crack the eggs into a bowl and season with salt and pepper, if using. Lightly beat with a fork until evenly mixed. Pour a little extra oil into the pan if needed, then pour in the eggs and cook for 5–6 minutes, or until they are almost set and the underside of the frittata is golden brown.

5. Grill the frittata for 3–4 minutes, or until the top is brown and the eggs are set. Cut into wedges and serve.

CHAPTER TWO

SIDES & SNACKS

CHARGRILLED
VEGETABLE BOWL

SERVES: *4* | **PREP:** *18 mins* | **COOK:** *35–40 mins*

INGREDIENTS

*1 yellow courgette, trimmed and
    sliced*

*1 green courgette, trimmed and
    sliced*

*100 g/3½ oz asparagus, trimmed
    and halved*

*1 red pepper, deseeded and
    chopped*

*1 yellow pepper, deseeded and
    chopped*

1 red onion, cut into 8 wedges

1 fennel bulb, trimmed and sliced

4 tbsp olive oil

2 tsp cumin seeds

*200 g/7 oz canned chickpeas,
    drained and rinsed*

50 g/1¾ oz walnuts

2 tbsp lemon juice

2 garlic cloves, crushed

2 tbsp tahini

3–4 tbsp water

½ tsp paprika

40 g/1½ oz watercress

4 fresh mint sprigs

salt and pepper (optional)

1. Preheat the oven to 200°C/400°F/Gas Mark 6.

2. Divide the chopped and sliced vegetables between two roasting
tins and drizzle each one with 1 tablespoon of the oil and 1 teaspoon
of the cumin seeds. Toss well to coat the vegetables with the oil.
Season with salt and pepper, if using.

3. Roast the vegetables in the preheated oven for 35–40 minutes until
they are beginning to char at the edges.

4. Meanwhile, place the chickpeas and walnuts in a food processor
and process until broken down.

5. With the machine running, add the lemon juice and then the
garlic, tahini and remaining oil. Add 3–4 tablespoons of water to
loosen and then add the paprika, and salt and pepper, if using.

6. Divide the watercress and roasted vegetables between four bowls,
then top with a dollop of the walnut hummus. Sprinkle with mint
sprigs to serve.

AUBERGINE PAPRIKA SALAD

SERVES: *4* | **PREP:** *15 mins* | **COOK:** *20 mins*

INGREDIENTS

2 aubergines

2 tbsp olive oil

2 red peppers, deseeded and cut into 6 pieces each

400 g/14 oz canned chickpeas, drained and rinsed

1 red onion, finely chopped

4 wholemeal pittas, to serve

DRESSING

3 tbsp olive oil

juice of ½ lemon

1 tsp ground coriander

1 tsp ground cumin

2 tsp smoked paprika

1 tsp stevia granules

small bunch of fresh coriander, leaves removed and reserved and stalks chopped

salt and pepper (optional)

1. Preheat the grill to high. Cut the aubergines lengthways into 1-cm/½-inch thick slices, brush with oil on both sides and arrange on a grill rack. Add the red pepper pieces. Cook under the preheated grill until the aubergines are charred in patches on the top side; turn over and cook until the aubergines are soft and the red pepper pieces are lightly cooked and slightly brown in places. Remove from the heat but do not switch off the grill.

2. Cut the aubergine slices into large bite-sized pieces and put into a shallow serving dish with the red peppers, chickpeas and onion.

3. To make the dressing, combine the oil, lemon juice, ground coriander, cumin, paprika and stevia granules with salt and pepper, if using, in a small bowl. Add the coriander stalks to the dressing and stir to combine. Spoon the dressing evenly over the salad and stir – it's best to do this while the vegetables are still warm.

4. Meanwhile, lightly toast the pittas under the grill. Scatter the salad with the coriander leaves and serve with the pittas.

RADICCHIO, ORANGE &
POMEGRANATE SIDE SALAD

SERVES: *4* | **PREP:** *10 mins* | **COOK:** *No cooking*

INGREDIENTS

1 small head of radicchio

100 g/3½ oz curly endive leaves

2 oranges, cut into segments

seeds from 1 small pomegranate

2 tbsp olive oil

2 tsp pomegranate molasses

2 tsp white wine vinegar

½ tsp salt

1 tsp pepper

1 tsp lightly crushed cumin seeds

3 tbsp chopped fresh flat-leaf
  parsley, to garnish

1. Roughly tear the radicchio leaves and arrange them on a serving platter with the curly endive leaves scattered around.

2. Place the orange segments on top of the radicchio leaves and scatter over the pomegranate seeds.

3. Whisk together the oil, molasses, vinegar, salt, pepper and cumin seeds and drizzle over the salad. Garnish with the parsley and serve the salad immediately.

ROASTED BROCCOLI WITH PINE NUTS & PARMESAN

SERVES: *4* | **PREP:** *20 mins* | **COOK:** *25 mins*

INGREDIENTS

1 head of broccoli, weighing 800 g/
1 lb 12 oz
6 tbsp olive oil
1 tsp sea salt
¼ tsp pepper
4 tbsp toasted pine nuts
grated zest of ½ lemon
25 g/1 oz Parmesan cheese
shavings
4 lemon wedges, to garnish

1. Preheat the oven to 230°C/450°F/Gas Mark 8. Cut off the broccoli crown where it meets the stalk. Remove the outer peel from the stalk. Slice the stalk crossways into 8-cm/3¼-inch pieces, then quarter each slice lengthways. Cut the crown into 4-cm/1½-inch wide wedges.

2. Put the broccoli wedges and stalks in a bowl. Sprinkle with the oil, salt and pepper, gently tossing to coat. Spread out in a large roasting tin. Cover tightly with foil and roast the broccoli on the bottom rack of the preheated oven for 10 minutes.

3. Remove the foil, then roast for a further 5–8 minutes until just starting to brown. Turn the stalks and wedges over, and roast for a further 3–5 minutes until tender.

4. Tip into a shallow warmed serving dish, together with any cooking juices. Sprinkle with the pine nuts and lemon zest, tossing to mix. Scatter the cheese shavings over the top.

5. Garnish the broccoli with lemon wedges and serve hot, warm or at room temperature.

GRIDDLED AUBERGINE &
BULGAR WHEAT SALAD

SERVES: *2* | **PREP:** *15 mins* | **COOK:** *10 mins*

INGREDIENTS

70 g/2½ oz bulgar wheat

150 ml/5 fl oz boiling water

2 tbsp chopped fresh parsley

1 tbsp chopped fresh mint

1 large aubergine

1 large courgette, cut into 1-cm/
  ½-inch slices

2 tbsp olive oil

1 tbsp lemon juice

½ tsp salt

½ tsp pepper

½ tsp smoked paprika

1½ tbsp toasted pine nuts

2 spring onions, chopped

1. Put the bulgar wheat into a heatproof bowl and pour over the water. Set aside for 15 minutes, then fluff up with a fork. Stir in the parsley and mint.

2. Meanwhile, cut the aubergine into 2-cm/¾-inch rounds, then cut each round in half. Brush the aubergine and courgette with the oil. Place a griddle pan over a high heat, then add the vegetables and cook for 8 minutes, turning halfway through, or until lightly charred and soft. Remove from the heat and sprinkle over the lemon juice, salt, pepper, paprika and any remaining oil.

3. Serve the vegetables on top of the bulgar wheat and garnish with the pine nuts and chopped spring onions.

SWEET POTATO FRIES

SERVES: *4* | **PREP:** *15 mins* | **COOK:** *20 mins*

INGREDIENTS

vegetable oil spray, for oiling
900 g/2 lb sweet potatoes
½ tsp salt
½ tsp ground cumin
¼ tsp cayenne pepper

1. Preheat the oven to 230°C/450°F/Gas Mark 8. Spray a large baking tray with vegetable oil spray.

2. Cut the sweet potatoes into 5-mm/¼-inch thick chips. Arrange them on the prepared tray in a single layer and spray them with vegetable oil spray.

3. Mix the salt, cumin and cayenne pepper together in a small bowl, then sprinkle the mixture evenly over the sweet potatoes and toss well together.

4. Bake in the preheated oven for 15–20 minutes, or until cooked through and lightly coloured. Serve hot.

STUFFED AUBERGINES

SERVES: *4* | **PREP:** *30 mins* | **COOK:** *50 mins*

INGREDIENTS

2 aubergines

1 tbsp virgin olive oil

1 small onion, finely chopped

2 garlic cloves, finely chopped

140 g/5 oz white quinoa

*350 ml/12 fl oz home-made
    vegetable stock*

*25 g/1 oz unblanched almonds,
    thinly sliced and toasted*

*2 tbsp finely chopped fresh mint,
    plus a few sprigs to garnish*

*85 g/3 oz feta cheese, drained and
    crumbled*

salt and pepper (optional)

1. Preheat the oven to 230°C/450°F/Gas Mark 8. Put the aubergines on a baking sheet and bake in the preheated oven for 15 minutes, or until soft. Leave to cool slightly. Do not switch off the oven.

2. Cut each aubergine in half lengthways and scoop out the flesh, leaving a 5-mm/¼-inch-thick border inside the skin so they hold their shape. Chop the flesh.

3. Heat the oil in a large, heavy-based frying pan over a medium–high heat. Add the onion and garlic and cook, stirring occasionally, for 5 minutes, or until soft. Add the quinoa, stock and aubergine flesh, and season with salt and pepper, if using. Reduce the heat to medium–low, cover and cook for 15 minutes, or until the quinoa is cooked through. Remove from the heat and stir in the sliced almonds, mint and half the feta cheese.

4. Divide the quinoa mixture equally between the aubergine skins and top with the remaining cheese. Bake for 10–15 minutes, or until the cheese is bubbling and beginning to brown. Garnish with the mint sprigs and serve.

ROAST CAULIFLOWER
WITH PARMESAN

SERVES: *4* | **PREP:** *10 mins* | **COOK:** *30 mins*

INGREDIENTS

1 head of cauliflower, cut into small
   florets
2 tbsp extra virgin rapeseed oil
¼ tsp salt
½ tsp pepper
1 tsp Italian seasoning
1 tsp garlic purée
1 tbsp lemon juice
5 tbsp freshly grated Parmesan
   cheese

1. Preheat the oven to 200°C/400°F/Gas Mark 6. Line a baking tray with baking paper.

2. Place the cauliflower florets in a bowl and toss with the oil, salt, pepper, Italian seasoning, garlic and lemon juice.

3. Transfer the cauliflower mixture to the prepared tray and roast in the preheated oven for 20 minutes, turning over halfway through the cooking time.

4. Sprinkle the cheese over the cauliflower and roast for a further 10 minutes, or until light golden and the cauliflower is tender when pierced with a sharp knife. Serve immediately.

BRAZILIAN GREENS WITH BLACK BEANS & ORANGES

SERVES: *4* | **PREP:** *25 mins* | **COOK:** *25 mins*

INGREDIENTS

1 large orange

3 tbsp olive oil

1 small onion, finely chopped

1 garlic clove, finely chopped

*1 fresh green chilli, deseeded
    and finely chopped*

*600 g/1 lb 5 oz kale,
    thick stalks removed and leaves
    sliced crossways*

*6–8 tbsp vegetable stock
    or chicken stock*

*400 g/14 oz canned black beans,
    drained and rinsed*

6 tbsp chopped fresh coriander

1 tbsp olive oil, for drizzling

salt and pepper (optional)

1. Using a sharp knife, cut a slice from the top and bottom of the orange. Remove the peel and white pith by cutting downwards, following the shape of the fruit as closely as possible. Working over a bowl, cut between the flesh and membrane of each segment and ease out the flesh. Slice each segment in half. Squeeze the membrane over the bowl to extract the juice.

2. Heat the oil in a large frying pan over a medium heat. Add the onion and fry for 5 minutes until soft. Add the garlic and chilli and fry for a further 2 minutes.

3. Gradually stir in the kale. Add a splash of stock, then cover and cook for 5–6 minutes, or until just wilted. Add more stock if the leaves start to look dry. Stir in the orange juice and any remaining stock. Season to taste with salt and pepper, if using, then cover and cook for 5 minutes, until the kale is tender.

4. Stir in the beans and the orange segments. Simmer, uncovered, for a few minutes to heat through. Stir in the coriander, drizzle with a little oil and serve immediately.

BUTTERNUT WEDGES WITH SAGE & PUMPKIN SEEDS

SERVES: *3* | **PREP:** *20 mins* | **COOK:** *35 mins*

INGREDIENTS

1 large butternut squash
1 tbsp olive oil
½ tsp chilli powder
12 fresh sage leaves, finely chopped
50 g/1¾ oz pumpkin seeds
salt and pepper (optional)

1. Preheat the oven to 200°C/400°F/Gas Mark 6. Prepare the butternut squash by washing any excess dirt from the skin and slicing off the very top and very bottom.

2. With a sharp knife and a steady hand, cut the squash into six long wedges. Scoop out any seeds and discard. Place the wedges on a baking tray. Brush with half the oil and sprinkle with the chilli powder. Roast in the preheated oven for 25 minutes.

3. Remove from the oven and brush with the remaining oil. Sprinkle over the sage and pumpkin seeds. Season with salt and pepper, if using, and return the wedges to the oven for a further 10 minutes. Serve immediately, garnished with extra pepper, if using.

SPICED CARROT MASH

SERVES: *4* | **PREP:** *20 mins, plus cooling* | **COOK:** *30–35 mins*

INGREDIENTS

1.25 kg/2 lb 12 oz carrots, cut in half lengthways

1 small garlic bulb, cloves peeled but left whole

1 tsp ground turmeric

1 tsp ground coriander

1 tsp ground cumin

2 tbsp olive oil

salt and pepper (optional)

2 tsp black onion seeds, to garnish

1 tbsp roughly chopped flat-leaf parsley, to garnish (optional)

1. Preheat the oven to 200°C/400°F/Gas Mark 6.

2. Place the carrots, garlic, turmeric, coriander and cumin in a large roasting tin. Drizzle over the oil and stir well until the carrots are thoroughly coated. Season with salt and pepper, if using.

3. Roast in the preheated oven for 30–35 minutes, or until soft. Turn once about halfway through, to ensure even cooking.

4. Remove from the oven and leave to cool slightly. Firmly mash the carrot mixture until you have a soft consistency, adding a touch of hot water if needed. Season to taste with salt and pepper, if using.

5. Serve immediately in a warmed serving dish, garnished with black onion seeds and parsley, if using.

MINTED BROAD BEAN BRUSCHETTA

SERVES: *4* | **PREP:** *15 mins* | **COOK:** *15 mins*

INGREDIENTS

400 g/14 oz shelled broad beans

4 tbsp extra virgin olive oil

juice of 1 lemon

15 g/½ oz fresh mint leaves,
*   chopped*

8 slices sourdough bread

2 garlic cloves, peeled, but left whole

125 g/4½ oz feta cheese

2 tbsp pumpkin seeds, toasted

salt and pepper (optional)

1. Bring a large saucepan of water to the boil. Add the broad beans and cook for 3 minutes. Drain, refresh under cold water and drain again. Remove the outer skin of the beans, if liked.

2. Use a fork to roughly mash the beans with 3 tablespoons of the oil and all the lemon juice, then stir through the mint. Season to taste with salt and pepper, if using.

3. Heat a griddle pan and cook the bread slices on both sides. Rub both sides of the bread with the garlic cloves.

4. Top each slice of bread with the broad bean mixture, then crumble over the cheese, sprinkle with the pumpkin seeds and drizzle with the remaining oil.

SWEET POTATO FALAFELS

MAKES: *16 falafels* | **PREP:** *30–35 mins, plus chilling* | **COOK:** *35–40 mins*

INGREDIENTS

2 (about 550 g/1 lb 4 oz) sweet
    potatoes, cut into chunks
3 tsp ground cumin
1 tsp ground coriander
1 tsp ground turmeric
3 tbsp olive oil
400 g/14 oz canned chickpeas,
    rinsed and drained
75 g/2¾ oz chickpea flour
25 g/1 oz fresh flat-leaf parsley,
    leaves picked
25 g/1 oz fresh coriander, leaves
    picked
1 tsp salt
100 g/3½ oz sesame seeds
100 g/3½ oz natural yogurt, to serve

1. Preheat the oven to 200°C/400°F/Gas Mark 6. Place the sweet potato chunks in a roasting tin. Sprinkle over 2 teaspoons of the cumin and all of the ground coriander and turmeric. Pour over 1 tablespoon of the oil and mix well so the sweet potatoes are coated in the spice paste. Make sure the chunks are spread in an even layer and roast in the preheated oven for 20 minutes.

2. Remove the sweet potatoes from the oven and transfer them to a food processor. Add the chickpeas, chickpea flour, parsley, coriander, salt and the remaining cumin. Blitz to a paste. Don't overwork the mixture – stop as soon as you have a paste. Transfer the mixture to a refrigerator and leave to chill for 15–20 minutes.

3. Preheat the oven again to 180°C/350°F/Gas Mark 4. Shape the cooled chickpea mixture into 16 golf-ball-sized pieces. Roll each ball in sesame seeds, drizzle with 1 tablespoon of the remaining oil and roast in the preheated oven for 15–20 minutes, turning the falafels over halfway through cooking. At the end of the cooking time, the sesame seeds should be golden.

4. Drizzle the hot falafels with the remaining oil and serve with the yogurt. Serve immediately or store in the refrigerator and eat chilled within 24 hours.

RED LENTIL &
SWEET POTATO PÂTÉ

SERVES: *4* | **PREP:** *15 mins, plus chilling* | **COOK:** *35 mins*

INGREDIENTS

2 tbsp olive oil

1 small onion, very finely chopped

2 garlic cloves, crushed

1¼ tsp sweet paprika

¼ tsp cayenne pepper

1 tsp pepper

1 sweet potato, about 250 g/9 oz
   peeled weight, cut into 1-cm/
   ½-inch cubes

150 g/5½ oz red lentils

350 ml/12 fl oz vegetable stock

juice of ½ small orange

¼ cucumber

2 wholemeal pittas

2 large celery sticks, cut into batons

salt (optional)

1. Place a frying pan over a medium–low heat and add half the oil. Add the onion and cook, stirring occasionally, for about 10 minutes, or until soft and golden.

2. Add the garlic, 1 teaspoon of the paprika, the cayenne pepper and pepper and cook for a further 2 minutes. Add the sweet potato, lentils and stock. Bring to a simmer and cook, uncovered, stirring occasionally, for 20 minutes, or until the potato and lentils are tender. You may need to add a little more liquid towards the end of the cooking time if the pan dries out.

3. Add the orange juice and salt to taste, if using. Mash the mixture to a smooth consistency, or to your liking, and spoon into a serving bowl. Chill in the refrigerator for 30 minutes, then drizzle with the remaining oil and sprinkle over the remaining paprika.

4. Cut the cucumber into quarters lengthways and remove the seeds with a sharp knife. Cut the cucumber into batons. Lightly toast the pittas and cut each one into six pieces. Serve the pâté with the pitta bread and the cucumber and celery batons.

CANNELLINI DIP
WITH CRUDITÉS

SERVES: *4* | **PREP:** *10 mins, plus chilling* | **COOK:** *No cooking*

INGREDIENTS

*400 g/14 oz canned cannellini
  beans, drained and rinsed*

2 garlic cloves, crushed

juice of ½ lemon

4 tbsp olive oil

½ tsp salt

1 tsp pepper

1 tsp smoked paprika

*3 tbsp finely chopped fresh flat-leaf
  parsley*

3 carrots, cut into batons

4 small celery sticks, cut into batons

4 radishes, quartered

1 yellow pepper, sliced

1. Place the beans in a food processor or blender with the garlic, lemon juice, oil, salt, pepper and half the paprika. Blend until completely smooth. If the dip is a little thick, beat in a little water, 1 teaspoon at a time, until you achieve the desired consistency.

2. Stir in the parsley and spoon the dip into four ramekins. Cover and chill in the refrigerator for 1–2 hours to allow the flavours to develop.

3. Sprinkle the remaining paprika over the dip and place the ramekins on four serving plates. Arrange the vegetables around the ramekins and serve.

HONEY & SPICE SNACKING NUTS

SERVES: 6 | **PREP:** 5–10 mins, plus cooling | **COOK:** 10 mins

INGREDIENTS

75 g/2¾ oz Brazil nuts
50 g/1¾ oz pecan nuts
50 g/1¾ oz cashew nuts
25 g/1 oz pumpkin seeds
1 tbsp sunflower oil
1½ tbsp clear honey
½ tsp ground cinnamon
½ tsp mixed spice
½ tsp pepper
½ tsp sweet paprika
¼ tsp salt

1. Line a baking tray with baking paper. Preheat the oven to 140°C/275°F/Gas Mark 1.

2. Combine all the ingredients in a bowl, except for ½ tablespoon of the honey, and then spread out on the prepared tray.

3. Place the tray on the middle shelf of the preheated oven and bake for 10 minutes. Remove from the oven and drizzle the remaining honey over the nuts. Leave to cool, then serve. Store in an airtight container for up to 1 week.

ROSEMARY, SEA SALT & SESAME POPCORN

SERVES: *4* | **PREP:** *10–15 mins* | **COOK:** *6–8 mins*

INGREDIENTS

40 g/1½ oz sesame seeds

2 tbsp olive oil

2 rosemary sprigs, torn into large
*   pieces*

200 g/7 oz popping corn

1 tsp sea salt

2 tbsp balsamic vinegar, or to taste

1. Add the sesame seeds to a large frying pan with 1 teaspoon of the oil, cover and cook over a medium heat for 2–3 minutes, shaking the pan from time to time, until the seeds are golden brown and beginning to pop. Scoop out of the pan into a bowl and wipe out the pan with a piece of kitchen paper.

2. Add the remaining oil and the rosemary to the pan and heat gently. Add the corn, cover with the lid and cook over a medium heat for 3–4 minutes, shaking the pan, until all the popcorn has popped. Remove from the heat and sprinkle with the toasted sesame seeds and season with the salt and vinegar. Discard the rosemary just before eating.

APPLE & CINNAMON CRISPS

SERVES: *4* | **PREP:** *20–25 mins, plus cooling* | **COOK:** *1½–2hrs*

INGREDIENTS

1 litre/1¾ pints water

1 tbsp sea salt

3 dessert apples, such as Braeburn
  or Gala

¼ tsp ground cinnamon

1. Preheat the oven to 110°C/225°F/Gas Mark ¼. Put the water and salt into a large mixing bowl and stir until the salt has dissolved.

2. Very thinly slice the apples, one at a time, with a sharp knife or mandolin, leaving the skin on and the core still in place, but removing any pips. Add each apple slice to the water. Turn to coat in the salt water, which will help prevent discoloration.

3. Drain the apple slices in a colander, then lightly pat dry with a clean tea towel. Arrange in a thin layer on a large rack so that the heat can circulate under the slices as well as over the tops.

4. Bake in the preheated oven for 1½–2 hours until the apple slices are dry and crisp. Loosen with a palette knife and transfer to a large plate or chopping board, then sprinkle with cinnamon. Leave to cool completely, then serve, or pack into an airtight plastic container and keep in the refrigerator for up to 2 days.

CHICKEN, KALE & CHIA SEED BITES

MAKES: *16 bites* | **PREP:** *20–25 mins, plus cooling* | **COOK:** *21 mins*

INGREDIENTS

2 x 125-g/4½-oz skinless, boneless
*   chicken breasts*
1 garlic clove, finely chopped
55 g/2 oz kale, shredded
115 g/4 oz light cream cheese
grated zest of 1 lemon
2 tsp chia seeds
salt and pepper (optional)

1. Place the chicken breasts in the top of a steamer half-filled with boiling water. Sprinkle over the garlic, season with salt and pepper, if using, cover and cook over a medium heat for 20 minutes, or until the juices run clear with no trace of pink when the chicken is pierced with a sharp knife.

2. Add the kale to the steamer and cook for 1 minute to soften it slightly.

3. Remove the steamer from the pan and leave to cool, then finely chop the chicken and kale.

4. Mix the cream cheese, lemon zest and chia seeds together, then stir in the chicken and kale. Taste and adjust the seasoning, if using.

5. Using two teaspoons, scoop spoonfuls of the mixture onto a plate, scraping off with the second spoon. Roll the mixture into balls, then pack into an airtight plastic container and store in the refrigerator for up to 2 days.

HOME-MADE SPICED PEANUT BUTTER

INGREDIENTS

200 g/7 oz unsalted peanuts

½ tsp salt

½ tsp paprika

½ tbsp groundnut oil

1. Place the nuts and salt in the bowl of a small food processor or chopper. Pulse, switching off every 20 seconds so that the machine does not overheat. Keep pulsing until the nuts progress from a crumble to a paste and then to a thick cream consistency.

2. Add the paprika and blend for a further 30 seconds, then drizzle in the oil and blend again.

3. Store the spiced peanut butter in a lidded jar or airtight plastic container in the refrigerator for up to 5 days.

FIG & OAT BITES

MAKES: *25 bites* | **PREP:** *20–25 mins, plus cooling* | **COOK:** *20 mins*

INGREDIENTS

450 g/1 lb soft dried figs

3 tbsp coconut oil, at room
  temperature

½ tsp ground ginger

½ tsp ground cinnamon

juice of 1 large orange

200 g/7 oz rolled oats

1 tbsp chia seeds

1. Preheat the oven to 180°C/350°F/Gas Mark 4. Line a 23-cm/9-inch square baking tin with baking paper.

2. Place the figs, oil, ginger and cinnamon in a food processor and pulse until roughly chopped. Add the orange juice and oats and pulse again until the mixture just comes together. If a little dry, add a touch more orange juice; if a little wet, stir through a few more oats. Add the chia seeds and pulse again very briefly.

3. Spoon the mixture into the prepared tin. Use the back of a greased spatula to push the mixture into the corners and spread it evenly.

4. Bake in the preheated oven for 20 minutes. Remove from the oven and, using a sharp knife, cut into 25 small squares. Leave to cool completely on a wire rack and then serve.

CHAPTER THREE

LUNCH

SALMON BURRITO BOWL

SERVES: *4* | **PREP:** *20 mins* | **COOK:** *25 mins*

INGREDIENTS

SALMON

1 tbsp coconut oil
2 garlic cloves, crushed
1 red onion, peeled and diced
1 celery stick, diced
1 red pepper, deseeded and diced
*400 g/14 oz canned red kidney
   beans, drained and rinsed*
200 g/7 oz long-grain rice
600 ml/1 pint vegetable stock
2 tbsp jerk paste
2 tbsp honey
*4 salmon fillets each weighing
   150 g/5½ oz*

MANGO SALSA

*1 large mango, peeled, stoned and
   diced*
½ red onion, finely diced
2 tbsp chopped fresh coriander
juice of 1 lime

1. To make the mango salsa, mix the mango, onion, coriander and lime juice together and leave to stand at room temperature.

2. Meanwhile, heat the oil in a large saucepan, add the garlic, onion, celery and red pepper and sauté for 4–5 minutes. Add the beans.

3. Add the rice and stock, bring to the boil, cover and simmer for about 15 minutes until tender and the liquid has been absorbed.

4. Meanwhile, mix the jerk paste and honey together. Preheat the grill to hot and line a baking tray with foil. Place the salmon fillets on the prepared tray and spread the jerk mixture over each one.

5. Cook the salmon under the grill for 8–10 minutes, turning once.

6. Serve the rice in warmed bowls, topped with a fillet of salmon and some mango salsa.

TOFU & EDAMAME
NOODLE BROTH BOWL

SERVES: *4* | **PREP:** *15 mins, plus marinating* | **COOK:** *15 mins*

INGREDIENTS

2 tbsp low-salt soy sauce

2 tbsp rice vinegar

1 tbsp mirin

250 g/9 oz firm silken tofu, cut into
12 pieces

15 g/½ oz cornflour

1 tbsp groundnut oil

1 litre/1¾ pints reduced-salt
vegetable stock

250 g/9 oz buckwheat soba noodles

125 g/4½ oz frozen edamame
beans

85 g/3 oz tenderstem broccoli stems

1 tbsp miso paste

½ tbsp sesame oil

6 spring onions, sliced

2.5-cm/1-inch piece fresh ginger,
peeled and finely chopped

1 red chilli, deseeded and thinly
sliced

4 tbsp fresh coriander leaves,
to garnish

1. Combine the soy sauce, vinegar and mirin in a small bowl. Place the tofu in a shallow non-metallic bowl in a single layer and spoon over the soy marinade. Leave to marinate for at least 30 minutes, turning once.

2. Scatter the cornflour on a plate. Remove the tofu from the marinade, reserving the marinade, and coat in the cornflour. Heat the groundnut oil in a large frying pan over a medium–high heat. Add the tofu to the pan and fry, turning once or twice, until golden and crisp all over. Remove with a slotted spatula, drain on kitchen paper, set aside and keep warm.

3. Put the stock into a saucepan with the reserved marinade, noodles, edamame beans and broccoli and bring to a simmer. Cook for 5 minutes, or until the noodles and vegetables are just tender. Stir in the miso paste.

4. Meanwhile, add the sesame oil to the frying pan and place over a high heat. Stir-fry the spring onions, ginger and chilli for 1 minute.

5. To serve, divide the noodle soup between four bowls, top with the tofu pieces and then the spring onion mixture. Garnish with the coriander leaves and serve immediately.

CHORIZO & KALE SOUP

SERVES: *6* | **PREP:** *15–20 mins* | **COOK:** *35 mins*

INGREDIENTS

3 tbsp olive oil
1 Spanish onion, finely chopped
2 garlic cloves, finely chopped
900 g/2 lb potatoes, diced
1.5 litres/2¾ pints vegetable stock
*125 g/4½ oz chorizo or other spicy
    sausage, thinly sliced*
*450 g/1 lb kale or Savoy cabbage,
    cored and shredded*
salt and pepper (optional)

1. Heat 2 tablespoons of the oil in a large saucepan. Add the onion and garlic and cook over a low heat, stirring occasionally, for 5 minutes until soft. Add the potatoes and cook, stirring constantly, for a further 3 minutes.

2. Increase the heat to medium, pour in the stock and bring to the boil. Reduce the heat, cover and cook for 10 minutes.

3. Meanwhile, heat the remaining oil in a frying pan. Add the chorizo and cook over a low heat, turning occasionally, for a few minutes until the fat runs. Remove from the pan with a slotted spoon and drain on kitchen paper.

4. Remove the soup from the heat and crush the potatoes with a potato masher. Return to the heat, add the kale and bring back to the boil. Reduce the heat and simmer for 5–6 minutes until tender.

5. Remove the pan from the heat and crush the potatoes again. Stir in the chorizo and season to taste with salt and pepper, if using. Ladle into warmed bowls and serve immediately.

PROTEIN RICE BOWL

SERVES: *2* | **PREP:** *25 mins* | **COOK:** *30 mins*

INGREDIENTS

150 g/5½ oz brown rice

2 large eggs

70 g/2½ oz spinach

4 spring onions, finely chopped

1 red chilli, deseeded and finely sliced

½ ripe avocado, sliced

2 tbsp roasted peanuts

VINAIGRETTE

2 tbsp olive oil

1 tsp Dijon mustard

1 tbsp cider vinegar

juice of ½ lemon

1. Place the rice in a large saucepan and cover with twice the volume of water. Bring to the boil and simmer for 25 minutes, or until the rice is tender and almost all the liquid has disappeared. Continue to simmer for a further few minutes if some liquid remains.

2. Meanwhile, cook your eggs. Bring a small saucepan of water to the boil. Carefully add the eggs to the pan and boil for 7 minutes – the whites will be cooked and the yolks should still be very slightly soft. Drain and pour cold water over the eggs to stop them cooking. When cool enough to handle, tap them on the work surface to crack the shells and peel them. Cut the eggs into quarters.

3. Stir the spinach, half the spring onions and a little of the chilli into the cooked rice.

4. To make the vinaigrette, whisk the oil, mustard, vinegar and lemon juice together. Pour the dressing over the warm rice and mix thoroughly to combine.

5. Divide the rice between two bowls and top each with the remaining spring onions, the avocado, the remaining chilli and the peanuts and egg quarters.

RAINBOW RICE
& BEAN BOWL

SERVES: *4* | **PREP:** *15–20 mins* | **COOK:** *10 mins*

INGREDIENTS

100 g/3½ oz brown basmati rice
100 g/3½ oz wild rice
400 g/14 oz canned mixed beans,
   drained and rinsed
200 g/7 oz frozen sweetcorn,
   thawed
100 g/3½ oz frozen peas, thawed
1 small red onion, finely sliced
55 g/2 oz pistachio nuts, chopped
1 large carrot, peeled and grated
1 large avocado, sliced
salt and pepper (optional)
fresh coriander leaves, to serve

DRESSING

grated zest and juice of 1 lime
2 tbsp extra virgin olive oil
1 tsp honey
1 red chilli, deseeded and diced
15 g/½ oz fresh mint leaves,
   chopped

1. Cook the rice according to the packet instructions.

2. Meanwhile, to make the dressing, whisk together the lime zest and juice, oil, honey, chilli and mint.

3. Drain the rice, place it in a large bowl and mix in the beans, sweetcorn, peas, onion, nuts and carrot. Stir in the dressing and season to taste with salt and pepper, if using.

4. Divide between four bowls, top with the avocado slices and sprinkle with coriander leaves to serve.

HOT-SMOKED SALMON
WITH CUCUMBER SALAD

SERVES: *2* | **PREP:** *10 mins, plus standing* | **COOK:** *No cooking*

INGREDIENTS

250 g/9 oz hot-smoked salmon
1 tbsp creamed horseradish
3 tbsp Greek-style natural yogurt
½ tsp pepper
fresh pea shoots, to garnish

CUCUMBER SALAD

10-cm/4-inch piece of cucumber,
    peeled and cut into thin strips
1 tsp caster sugar
1 tbsp chopped fresh dill
1 tbsp white wine vinegar

1. To make the salad, put the cucumber into a shallow non-metallic bowl. Stir the sugar and dill into the vinegar, then spoon this mixture evenly over the cucumber. Set aside for 30 minutes.

2. Meanwhile, bring the salmon to room temperature if it has been in the refrigerator. Cut into eight pieces and arrange four pieces on each serving plate.

3. Beat the horseradish with the yogurt in a small bowl. Stir in the pepper and spoon the mixture over the salmon. Divide the cucumber salad between the plates, spooning over any dressing remaining in the cucumber dish.

4. Garnish with the pea shoots and serve.

TUNA &
ASPARAGUS SALAD

SERVES: *4* | **PREP:** *10 mins* | **COOK:** *25 mins*

INGREDIENTS

175 g/6 oz quinoa, rinsed

8 quail eggs

6 sprays cooking oil spray

24 asparagus spears, woody stems
  discarded

4 tuna steaks, each weighing
  100 g/3½ oz

2 tbsp olive oil

½ tbsp white wine vinegar

½ tsp Dijon mustard

½ tsp sugar

½ tsp salt

½ tsp pepper

12 cherry tomatoes, halved

4 small spring onions, finely
  chopped, to garnish

1. Bring a saucepan of water to the boil and add the quinoa. Cook for 15–18 minutes, or until just tender. Drain and set aside.

2. Meanwhile, bring a separate saucepan of water to the boil and add the eggs. Cook for 3 minutes, then drain and rinse in cold water to cool. When the eggs are cool enough to handle, peel and halve them.

3. Place a ridged griddle pan over a high heat and spray with 2 sprays of cooking spray. Add the asparagus spears and cook, turning once, for 4 minutes, or until they are slightly charred and just tender.

4. Spray the tuna steaks with the remaining cooking oil spray and cook in the pan for 1½ minutes. Turn and cook for a further minute, or to your liking. Transfer to a plate and leave to rest for 2 minutes.

5. Beat together the olive oil, vinegar, mustard, sugar, salt and pepper in a small bowl. Stir two thirds of this mixture into the quinoa.

6. Cut each tuna steak into three pieces. Divide the quinoa between four serving plates and top evenly with the tuna pieces, asparagus, eggs and tomatoes. Drizzle the remaining dressing over the top and garnish with the spring onions.

MASHED AVOCADO
& QUINOA WRAP

SERVES: *4* | **PREP:** *20 mins* | **COOK:** *15–18 mins*

INGREDIENTS

175 g/6 oz quinoa
400 ml/14 fl oz vegetable stock
1 large ripe avocado, stoned and
*   peeled*
½ tsp smoked paprika
2 garlic cloves, crushed
finely grated zest and juice of
*   1 lemon*
4 wholemeal tortillas
50 g/1¾ oz baby spinach
150 g/5½ oz red cabbage, finely
*   sliced*
salt and pepper (optional)

1. Place the quinoa and stock in a small saucepan over a medium heat and simmer, covered, for 15–18 minutes, or until the stock has been fully absorbed. Set aside to cool.

2. Meanwhile gently mash the avocado flesh with the smoked paprika, garlic, lemon zest and just enough lemon juice to make a thick consistency.

3. Spread the mashed avocado down the centre of each tortilla and then top with the warm quinoa, spinach and red cabbage. Season with salt and pepper, if using. Tuck in the ends, tightly fold or roll into a wrap and serve immediately.

SKINNY TURKEY
& EGG SANDWICHES

SERVES: *2* | **PREP:** *20 mins* | **COOK:** *10–14 mins*

INGREDIENTS

½ red onion, peeled and sliced into
  whole rounds
2 thin turkey steaks or escalopes
  (about 90–100 g/3¼–3½ oz)
½ tsp all-purpose seasoning
¼ tsp smoked paprika
4 thick slices of wholegrain bread
55 g/2 oz low-fat soft cheese
2 hard-boiled eggs, whites only,
  chopped
2 tomatoes, thinly sliced
1 lemon wedge
15 g/½ oz rocket leaves
salt and pepper (optional)

1. Preheat a ridged griddle pan until smoking hot. Add the onion rounds and cook for 2–3 minutes on each side until soft and lightly charred. Transfer to a plate.

2. Wipe the turkey steaks with kitchen paper. Sprinkle with the all-purpose seasoning and paprika and rub into the meat. Arrange on the pan and cook for 3 minutes without moving them, until lightly charred underneath. Turn and cook for 2–3 minutes on the other side until thoroughly cooked through.

3. Spread the bread with the soft cheese. Cover two slices with the chopped egg white and tomato slices. Cut the turkey steaks in half, arrange on top and squeeze over a little lemon juice. Divide the rocket leaves between the sandwiches and season to taste with salt and pepper, if using. Top with the remaining bread, cut in half and serve immediately.

RED PEPPER HUMMUS, ROCKET & ARTICHOKE WRAPS

SERVES: *4* | **PREP:** *10 mins, plus cooling* | **COOK:** *5–10 mins*

INGREDIENTS

1 large red pepper, deseeded and
*   quartered*
400 g/14 oz canned chickpeas,
*   drained and rinsed*
2 tbsp lemon juice
2 tbsp tahini
4 wholemeal tortillas
40 g/1½ oz rocket leaves
200 g/7 oz artichoke hearts in oil,
*   drained and quartered*
salt and pepper (optional)

1. Preheat a grill to hot. Place the pepper quarters cut side down on a grill pan and cook under the preheated grill for 4–6 minutes, or until the skins are blackened and charred. Put the peppers in a polythene bag, seal and leave to cool.

2. Remove the skin from the pepper quarters and place the flesh in a food processor with the chickpeas, lemon juice and tahini. Process until almost smooth. Season to taste with salt and pepper, if using.

3. Divide the hummus between the tortillas, placing the hummus down the centre of each wrap. Top with the rocket leaves and artichoke hearts.

4. Fold the tortilla sides over to enclose the filling and serve.

TURKEY, MOZZARELLA & PEPPER PANINI

SERVES: *4* | **PREP:** *10 mins, plus cooling* | **COOK:** *10 mins*

INGREDIENTS

* red peppers, halved and deseeded
* ciabatta rolls
* 00 g/7 oz roast turkey breast, sliced
* 25 g/4½ oz half-fat mozzarella cheese, sliced
* andful of basil leaves
* tbsp sweet chilli sauce

1. Preheat a grill to hot. Place the red peppers cut side down on a grill pan and cook under the preheated grill for 4–6 minutes, or until the skins are blackened and charred. Put the peppers in a polythene bag, seal and leave to cool. Remove the skins once cool.

2. Split the rolls open and arrange the turkey on the bottom halves. Top with the cheese and basil. Drizzle with chilli sauce.

3. Thickly slice the peppers, then arrange over the other ingredients in the rolls.

4. Place a griddle pan over a high heat and cook the panini, pressing down lightly with a fish slice, or place under a hot grill until golden brown. Serve immediately.

WHOLEWHEAT SPINACH, PEA & FETA TART

SERVES: 6 | **PREP:** *20 mins, plus chilling* | **COOK:** *1 hour 10 mins*

INGREDIENTS

15 g/½ oz unsalted butter
3 spring onions, thinly sliced
200 g/7 oz baby spinach
100 g/3½ oz shelled peas
3 eggs
250 ml/9 fl oz milk
100 g/3½ oz feta cheese, drained
    and finely crumbled
115 g/4 oz cherry tomatoes

PASTRY

115 g/4 oz unsalted butter, cut into
    cubes
225 g/8 oz wholemeal plain flour,
    plus extra for dusting
2 eggs, beaten

1. To make the pastry, put the butter and flour in a mixing bowl. Rub the butter into the flour until it resembles fine crumbs. Mix in enough egg to make a soft dough. Dust a work surface with flour. Knead the pastry, then roll it out to a little larger than a 25-cm/10-inch loose-based tart tin. Lift the pastry over the rolling pin, ease it into the tin and press it into the sides. Trim the pastry so that it stands a little above the top of the tin, then prick the base with a fork. Cover the pastry case with clingfilm and chill in the refrigerator for 30 minutes. Preheat the oven to 190°C/375°F/Gas Mark 5.

2. To make the filling, melt the butter in a frying pan over a medium heat. Add the spring onions and cook for 2–3 minutes, or until softened. Add the spinach, turn the heat to high, and cook, stirring, until wilted. Set aside to cool. Cook the peas in a saucepan of boiling water for 2 minutes. Drain, then plunge into iced water and drain again. Crack the eggs into a jug, add the milk and beat with a fork.

3. Line the pastry case with a sheet of baking paper, fill with baking beans and place on a baking sheet. Bake in the preheated oven for 10 minutes, then remove the paper and beans and bake for a further 5 minutes, or until the base of the tart is crisp and dry.

4. Drain any cooking juices from the spring onions and spinach into the eggs. Put the onion mixture in the pastry case, add the peas, then sprinkle over the cheese. Fork the eggs and milk together once more, then pour into the tart case and dot the tomatoes over the top. Bake for 40–50 minutes, or until set and golden. Leave to cool for 20 minutes, then serve.

TURKEY GOUJONS WITH
RED CABBAGE & KALE SLAW

SERVES: *4* | **PREP:** *20 mins* | **COOK:** *15 mins*

INGREDIENTS

70 g/2½ oz linseeds
40 g/1½ oz sesame seeds
2 eggs
450 g/1 lb skinless boneless turkey
  breast, thinly sliced
3 tbsp virgin olive oil
salt and pepper (optional)

RED CABBAGE & KALE SLAW

115 g/4 oz red cabbage, thinly
  shredded
25 g/1 oz kale thinly shredded
1 carrot, coarsely grated
1 dessert apple, cored and roughly
  grated
1 tsp caraway seeds
60 g/2¼ oz Greek-style natural
  yogurt
salt and pepper (optional)

1. Preheat the oven to 220°C/425°F/Gas Mark 7 and put a large baking sheet in it to heat.

2. To make the slaw, put the cabbage, kale and carrot in a bowl and mix well. Add the apple, caraway seeds and yogurt, season with salt and pepper, if using, and mix well. Cover and chill in the refrigerator until needed.

3. Put the linseeds in a spice mill or blender and process until roughly ground. Add the sesame seeds and process for a few seconds. Tip the mixture out onto a plate. Crack the eggs into a dish, season with salt and pepper, if using, and lightly beat with a fork.

4. Dip each turkey slice into the eggs, then lift it out with a fork and dip both sides into the seed mixture to coat. Brush the hot baking sheet with a little oil, add the turkey slices in a single layer, then drizzle with a little extra oil.

5. Bake the turkey in the preheated oven, turning the slices once and moving them from the corners into the centre of the baking sheet, for 15 minutes, or until golden brown and cooked through. Cut one of the larger turkey goujons in half to check that the meat is no longer pink. Any juices that run out should be clear and piping hot with steam rising. Serve the goujons with the slaw.

MOROCCAN MEATBALLS

SERVES: *4* | **PREP:** *35 mins* | **COOK:** *15 mins*

INGREDIENTS

olive oil spray, for oiling
450 g/1 lb fresh lamb mince
½ small onion, finely chopped
1 garlic clove, finely chopped
1½ tsp ground cumin
1½ tsp salt
½ tsp pepper
¼ tsp ground cinnamon
1 egg
10 g/¼ oz fresh breadcrumbs
4 pittas
1 cucumber, diced
2 tbsp chopped fresh flat-leaf
  parsley
140 g/5 oz cherry tomatoes, halved
juice of 1 lemon
lemon wedges, to serve

YOGURT MINT SAUCE

10 g/¼ oz fresh mint leaves
280 g/10 oz natural yogurt
juice of ½ lemon
½ tsp salt
¼ tsp cayenne pepper

1. Preheat the oven to 190°C/375°F/Gas Mark 5 and spray a large baking sheet with oil. Put the lamb, onion, garlic, cumin, 1 teaspoon of the salt, the pepper, cinnamon, egg and breadcrumbs into a large bowl, mix well to combine and shape into 2.5-cm/1-inch balls.

2. Place the meatballs on the prepared baking sheet and spray with oil. Bake in the preheated oven for 15 minutes until cooked through.

3. Meanwhile, wrap the pittas in foil and put them in the oven. To make the sauce, finely chop the mint. Put the mint into a small bowl with the remaining ingredients and stir well.

4. To make the salad, put the cucumber, parsley and tomatoes into a medium-sized bowl and mix to combine. Add the lemon juice and the remaining ½ teaspoon of salt and stir to combine.

5. Remove the meatballs and bread from the oven. Cut the pittas in half. Stuff a few meatballs into each half and spoon in some of the sauce. Serve two halves per person with the salad and lemon wedges.

CHICKEN SATAY
SKEWERS

SERVES: *4* | **PREP:** *25–30 mins, plus marinating* | **COOK:** *12–15 mins*

INGREDIENTS

4 skinless, boneless chicken breasts,
about 115 g/4 oz each, cut into
2-cm/¾-inch cubes

4 tbsp soy sauce

1 tbsp cornflour

2 garlic cloves, finely chopped

2.5-cm/1-inch piece fresh ginger,
peeled and finely chopped

1 cucumber, diced, to serve

PEANUT SAUCE

2 tbsp groundnut or vegetable oil

½ onion, finely chopped

1 garlic clove, finely chopped

4 tbsp crunchy peanut butter

4–5 tbsp water

½ tsp chilli powder

1. Put the chicken cubes in a shallow dish. Mix the soy sauce, cornflour, garlic and ginger together in a small bowl and pour over the chicken. Cover and leave to marinate in the refrigerator for at least 2 hours.

2. Meanwhile, soak 12 wooden skewers in cold water for at least 30 minutes. Preheat the grill and thread the chicken pieces onto the wooden skewers. Transfer the skewers to a grill pan and cook under a preheated grill for 3–4 minutes. Turn the skewers over and cook for a further 3–4 minutes, or until cooked through and there are no remaining traces of pink or red when cut into with a sharp knife.

3. Meanwhile, to make the sauce, heat the oil in a saucepan, add the onion and garlic and cook over a medium heat, stirring frequently, for 3–4 minutes until soft. Add the peanut butter, water and chilli powder and simmer for 2–3 minutes. Serve the skewers immediately with the warm sauce and diced cucumber.

LOADED SWEET POTATOES

SERVES: *4* | **PREP:** *20–25 mins* | **COOK:** *50–55 mins*

INGREDIENTS

4 small sweet potatoes, scrubbed
1 tbsp olive oil
1 small onion, chopped
1 garlic clove, finely chopped
1 tsp ground coriander
½ tsp ground cumin
200 g/7 oz tomatoes, peeled and
*   diced*
2 tsp tomato purée
200 g/7 oz canned chickpeas,
*   drained and rinsed*
4 tbsp chopped fresh coriander
115 g/4 oz fat-free Greek-style
*   natural yogurt*
salt and pepper (optional)

1. Preheat the oven to 190°C/375°F/Gas Mark 5. Prick the potatoes with a fork, put them on a baking sheet and bake in the preheated oven for 45–50 minutes, or until they feel soft when squeezed.

2. Meanwhile, heat the oil in a small frying pan, add the onion and fry over a medium heat for 4–5 minutes until soft. Stir in the garlic, ground coriander and cumin, and cook for a further minute.

3. Mix in the tomatoes, tomato purée and chickpeas, then season with a little salt and pepper, if using. Cover and cook for 10 minutes, then remove from the heat and set aside.

4. Transfer the potatoes to a serving plate, slit each along its length and open out slightly. Reheat the chickpeas and spoon them over the potatoes. Mix half the fresh coriander into the yogurt and spoon over the chickpeas. Sprinkle with the remaining fresh coriander and serve the potatoes immediately.

LENTIL & GOAT'S CHEESE TOMATOES

SERVES: *4* | **PREP:** *15 mins* | **COOK:** *35–45 mins*

INGREDIENTS

55 g/2 oz dried Puy lentils
4 beef tomatoes
1 tbsp olive oil
2 large shallots, finely chopped
1 garlic clove, crushed
1 tbsp chopped fresh thyme
100 g/3½ oz hard goat's cheese,
*   diced*
salt and pepper (optional)
sliced cucumber and salad leaves,
*   to serve*

1. Bring a small saucepan of water to the boil over a medium–high heat. Add the lentils, bring back to the boil and cook for 20–25 minutes, or until tender. Drain well.

2. Meanwhile, preheat the oven to 200°C/400°F/Gas Mark 6. Cut a slice from the top of each tomato and set aside. Scoop out the pulp from the centre and roughly chop.

3. Heat the oil in a frying pan over a medium heat, add the shallots and fry, stirring, for 3–4 minutes to soften. Add the garlic and chopped tomato pulp and cook for a further 3–4 minutes, or until any excess moisture has evaporated.

4. Place the tomatoes in a shallow baking dish. Stir the lentils and thyme into the pan and season to taste with salt and pepper, if using. Stir in the cheese, then spoon the mixture into the tomatoes.

5. Replace the lids on the tomatoes and bake in the preheated oven for 15–20 minutes, or until tender. Serve immediately with sliced cucumber and salad leaves.

KALE & GREEN GARLIC BRUSCHETTA

SERVES: *4* | **PREP:** *25 mins* | **COOK:** *25 mins*

INGREDIENTS

1 green garlic bulb

3 tbsp olive oil

4 slices sourdough bread with mixed or sprouted seeds, total weight 250 g/9 oz

85 g/3 oz shredded kale, rinsed well and drained

1 tbsp balsamic vinegar

2 tsp pomegranate molasses

salt and pepper (optional)

1. Preheat the oven to 190°C/375°F/Gas Mark 5. Put the garlic bulb on a piece of foil, drizzle with 1 tablespoon of the oil, then wrap the foil around it and seal well. Put on a baking sheet and roast in the preheated oven for 20 minutes, or until it feels soft when squeezed.

2. Meanwhile, preheat a ridged griddle pan. Cut the bread slices in half, brush one side of each with a little oil, then cook, oiled side down, in the hot pan for 2 minutes. Brush the top with the remaining oil, then turn and cook the second side until golden brown.

3. Unwrap the garlic, peel away the outer casing from the bulb, separate the cloves, then remove any of the tougher skins. Crush the creamy soft garlic to a coarse paste using a pestle and mortar. Mix the paste with any juices from the foil, then thinly spread on the griddled bread and keep warm.

4. Heat a dry, non-stick frying pan, add the kale and cook over a medium heat for 2–3 minutes until just wilted. Mix in the vinegar, molasses and a little salt and pepper, if using. Arrange the bruschetta on a chopping board, spoon over the kale and serve.

HAM & SWEET POTATO HASH

SERVES: *4* | **PREP:** *15 mins* | **COOK:** *35 mins*

INGREDIENTS

250 g/9 oz floury potatoes, such as
Maris Piper, cut into 2-cm/
¾-inch cubes
2 tbsp water
2 tbsp extra virgin rapeseed oil
1 small red onion, very finely
chopped
1 garlic clove, finely chopped
500 g/1 lb 2 oz sweet potatoes, cut
into 1-cm/½-inch cubes
200 g/7 oz lean cooked ham, diced
100 g/3½ oz canned chickpeas,
drained and rinsed
1 tsp ground cumin seeds
1 tsp pepper
1 tsp dried chilli flakes (optional)
salt (optional)

1. Place the floury potato cubes and the water in a microwaveable bowl and microwave on High for 4 minutes, or until partly cooked. Drain and dry on kitchen paper.

2. Place a large non-stick frying pan over a medium heat and add the oil. Add the onion and fry, stirring occasionally, for 5 minutes until soft and beginning to brown. Add the garlic and stir for 30 seconds.

3. Add the floury and sweet potato cubes to the pan and cook, gently stirring occasionally, for 10 minutes. Stir in the ham and cook for a further 5 minutes. Check that the vegetables are tender when pierced with a sharp knife and nicely golden on the outside, and that the ham has a little colour too.

4. Stir in the chickpeas, cumin, pepper, chilli flakes, if using, and salt, if using. Cook for a further 3–5 minutes, or until everything is warmed through, then serve immediately.

CRAYFISH CAKES WITH AVOCADO & CHILLI MASH

SERVES: 2 | **PREP:** *15 mins, plus optional chilling* | **COOK:** *10 mins*

INGREDIENTS

25 g/1 oz wholemeal breadcrumbs

½ tsp pepper

2 tbsp finely chopped fresh flat-leaf parsley

200 g/7 oz peeled and cooked crayfish tails, roughly chopped

50 g/1¾ oz ready-roasted red pepper from a jar, drained and chopped

1 tsp medium-hot peri peri sauce

1 tbsp extra-light mayonnaise

1 small egg white, beaten

plain flour, for dusting

6 sprays cooking oil spray

AVOCADO & CHILLI MASH

1 ripe avocado, sliced

1 small fresh red chilli, deseeded and finely chopped

1 spring onion, finely chopped

½ tsp smoked paprika

juice of ¼ lime

1. Put the breadcrumbs, pepper and parsley into a bowl and stir well to combine.

2. In a separate bowl, combine the crayfish tails, red pepper, peri peri sauce and mayonnaise. Stir the breadcrumb mixture into the crayfish mixture and mix well.

3. Add the beaten egg white and mix to a moderately firm mixture – the cakes will firm up more once they are cooked. Divide into four rough rounds and sprinkle with flour. If you have time, chill for up to 1 hour.

4. To make the mash, place the avocado slices in a bowl and roughly mash with a fork. Stir in the chilli, spring onion, paprika and lime juice

5. Spray a non-stick frying pan with the cooking oil spray and place over a medium–high heat. Add the crayfish cakes and cook for 2–3 minutes, or until the underside is crisp and golden. Turn and cook for a further 2–3 minutes, or until cooked through. Serve the cakes immediately with the avocado mash on the side.

CHAPTER FOUR

DINNER

GRILLED CAULIFLOWER STEAKS WITH KALE SLAW

SERVES: *4* | **PREP:** *20 mins, plus standing* | **COOK:** *15 mins*

INGREDIENTS
KALE SLAW
125 g/4½ oz tender kale leaves, shredded

2 carrots, grated

1 small red onion, thinly sliced

2 tbsp extra virgin rapeseed oil

1 tsp Dijon mustard

½ tbsp cider vinegar

2 tsp maple syrup

1 tbsp pumpkin seeds

1 tbsp sunflower seeds

sea salt and pepper (optional)

CAULIFLOWER STEAKS
2 heads of cauliflower

3 tbsp extra virgin rapeseed oil

juice of ½ lime

1 tsp sweet paprika

1 large garlic clove, crushed

½ tsp sea salt

½ tsp pepper

1. To make the slaw, combine the kale, carrot and onion in a serving bowl. In a small bowl, thoroughly mix the oil, mustard, vinegar, maple syrup and salt and pepper, if using, together and stir into the slaw. Cover and set aside to rest for up to 1 hour. Before serving, sprinkle the seeds over the slaw.

2. To make the cauliflower steaks, preheat the grill to medium–hot. Meanwhile, remove the leaves from the cauliflower and cut the stalk across the base so it will sit firmly on your chopping board. Using a very sharp knife, cut down vertically about 5 cm/2 inches through the first cauliflower. Remove the florets that fall and repeat on the other side so you are left with the firm central piece of the vegetable. Slice through the cauliflower and stalk to produce 'steaks' that are around 2–2.5 cm/¾–1 inch thick. You should get two steaks from each cauliflower.

3. Cover the rack of a large grill pan with foil and place the steaks on top. Combine the oil, lime juice, paprika, garlic, salt and pepper in a small bowl and brush the steaks all over with this mixture. Grill the steaks about 5 cm/2 inches from the heat source for 8 minutes, or until the steaks are slightly browned.

4. Turn the steaks over carefully with a large metal spatula and brush again with any remaining oil mixture and any juices that have collected on the foil. Grill for a further 6 minutes, or until the steaks are well coloured and just tender when pierced with a sharp knife. Serve immediately with the kale slaw.

BUTTERNUT SQUASH BOWL

SERVES: *4* | **PREP:** *20 mins* | **COOK:** *1 hour 10 mins*

INGREDIENTS

2 butternut squash
2 tbsp olive oil
75 g/2½ oz brown basmati rice
75 g/2½ oz wild rice
1 tsp coconut oil
4 spring onions, trimmed and sliced
*3-cm/1¼-inch piece fresh ginger,
    grated*
*1 lemon grass stalk, trimmed and
    finely sliced*
1 tbsp Thai green curry paste
*400 ml/14 fl oz canned coconut
    milk*
400 g/14 oz canned green lentils
100 g/3½ oz cavolo nero
1 tbsp golden sesame seeds
1 tbsp black sesame seeds
fresh coriander leaves, to garnish

1. Preheat the oven to 200°C/400°F/Gas Mark 6.

2. Halve the squash, scoop out the seeds and score the flesh with a sharp knife.

3. Place the four squash halves on a baking tray and drizzle with olive oil. Roast in the preheated oven for 40 minutes. Meanwhile, cook the rice according to the packet instructions.

4. While the rice is cooking, heat the coconut oil in a frying pan. Add the spring onions, ginger and lemon grass and cook for 1 minute, then stir in the curry paste and cook for a further minute.

5. Add the coconut milk and lentils and bring to the boil. Simmer for 15 minutes.

6. Drain the rice and add to the lentil mixture with the cavolo nero. Simmer for 3–4 minutes.

7. Take the squash out of the oven and divide the lentil and rice mixture between the four halves.

8. Sprinkle with the sesame seeds and bake for a further 10 minutes. Sprinkle with coriander leaves and serve.

COURGETTE SPAGHETTI

SERVES: *2* | **PREP:** *30 mins* | **COOK:** *25–30 mins*

INGREDIENTS

150 g/5½ oz cherry tomatoes
4 garlic cloves, sliced
1 tbsp olive oil
50 g/1¾ oz sunflower seeds
2 large courgettes
2 tbsp fresh pesto
70 g/2½ oz feta cheese, crumbled
salt and pepper (optional)
chopped fresh basil, to garnish

1. Preheat the oven to 200°C/400°F/Gas Mark 6. Place the tomatoes and garlic in a small roasting tin and drizzle over the oil. Shake well to coat and bake in the preheated oven for 20 minutes.

2. Meanwhile, place a dry frying pan over a medium heat. Add the sunflower seeds and fry for 3–4 minutes, or until the seeds are just toasted. Set aside.

3. To make the courgette spaghetti, lay a box grater on its side and grate the length of the courgette into long strands.

4. Bring a saucepan of water to the boil and add the courgette strips. Cook for 1–2 minutes before draining thoroughly in a colander, gently squeezing any excess water away with the back of a spoon. Return the spaghetti to the pan and stir through the pesto. Season with salt and pepper, if using.

5. Stir two thirds of the roasted tomato mixture, half the sunflower seeds and half the feta cheese into the spaghetti. Divide the mixture between two warmed plates. Top with the sunflower seeds and cheese. Garnish with the basil and serve immediately.

SPICY STUFFED PEPPERS WITH CHICKPEAS

SERVES: *4* | **PREP:** *10 mins, plus standing* | **COOK:** *35 mins*

INGREDIENTS

12 sprays cooking oil spray

2 large red peppers

2 large yellow peppers

1 vegetable stock cube

85 g/3 oz bulgar wheat

*125 g/4½ oz canned chickpeas,
   drained and rinsed*

25 g/1 oz flaked almonds, toasted

25 g/1 oz raisins

*4 large sun-dried tomatoes,
   chopped*

4 spring onions, finely chopped

½ tsp smoked paprika

3 tbsp chopped fresh basil

*50 g/1¾ oz feta cheese, finely
   crumbled*

1. Preheat the oven to 190°C/375°F/Gas Mark 5. Spray a baking tray with 4 sprays of cooking oil spray. Halve the red peppers and yellow peppers from stalk to base and deseed. Place cut side down on the prepared tray and roast in the preheated oven for 20 minutes.

2. Meanwhile, prepare the bulgar wheat. Dissolve the stock cube in 175 ml/6 fl oz boiling water in a heatproof bowl and stir in the bulgar wheat. Set aside for 15 minutes, then fluff up with a fork.

3. Add the chickpeas, almonds, raisins, tomatoes, spring onion, paprika and basil to the bulgar wheat and stir well to combine.

4. Remove the peppers from the oven and stuff with the bulgar wheat mixture. Sprinkle a little cheese over the top of each stuffed pepper and spray with cooking oil spray. Roast for a further 15 minutes, or until the tops are light golden and the peppers are tender when pierced with a sharp knife. Serve immediately.

WHOLE BAKED CAULIFLOWER

SERVES: *4* | **PREP:** *20–25 mins* | **COOK:** *1 hour*

INGREDIENTS

1 tbsp olive oil

2 onions, finely sliced

4 garlic cloves, chopped

2 tbsp red wine vinegar

pinch of soft brown sugar

70 g/2½ oz black olives, stoned

2 tbsp capers

3 tbsp roughly chopped fresh basil

*800 g/1 lb 12 oz canned chopped
    tomatoes*

*400 g/14 oz canned butter beans,
    drained and rinsed*

150 ml/5 fl oz vegetable stock

1 large cauliflower, leaves trimmed

salt and pepper (optional)

*2 tbsp fresh basil sprigs, to garnish
    (optional)*

1. Heat the oil in a saucepan that is large enough to fit the whole head of cauliflower.

2. Add the onions and garlic and fry over a medium heat until soft and translucent. Stir in the vinegar, sugar, olives, capers and basil and heat through for a further 2–3 minutes. Pour in the tomatoes, butter beans and stock. Stir well and bring the tomato mixture to a simmer for 5–6 minutes, stirring occasionally.

3. Sit the cauliflower head upside down on a chopping board and, using a sharp knife, carefully cut away the tough stem. Place the cauliflower in the centre of the tomato sauce, pushing it down so half is covered by the sauce. Season with salt and pepper, if using.

4. Reduce the heat to low, cover and simmer for approximately 45 minutes, or until the cauliflower is tender. Carefully stir once or twice during cooking to prevent the sauce catching on the base of the pan. Serve immediately, garnished with basil, if using.

BAKED SALMON WITH SWEET POTATO & CUCUMBER RIBBONS

SERVES: *4* | **PREP:** *15 mins* | **COOK:** *15–20 mins*

INGREDIENTS

2 sweet potatoes

1½ tbsp extra virgin rapeseed oil

½ tsp sea salt

½ tsp pepper

1 cucumber, topped and tailed

1 tbsp white wine vinegar

1 tsp mild-flavoured clear honey,
*   such as acacia*

4 thick salmon fillets, about
*   125 g/4½ oz each*

2 tsp crushed cumin seeds

1 tbsp chopped fresh dill, to garnish

1. Preheat the oven to 190°C/375°F/Gas Mark 5. Slice the sweet potatoes lengthways into long, thin ribbons using a vegetable peeler, the side of a box grater or a spiraliser. Toss the ribbons in a bowl with half the oil and half the salt and pepper, then arrange on a baking tray. Place the tray near the top of the preheated oven and bake for 6 minutes. Do not switch off the oven.

2. Meanwhile, slice the cucumber into long, thin ribbons using a vegetable peeler, the side of a box grater or a spiralizer. Place the ribbons in a bowl. Mix the vinegar and honey together in a small bowl, then sprinkle the mixture over the cucumber ribbons and stir gently to combine.

3. Place the salmon fillets on a baking tray, brush with the remaining oil, sprinkle with the crushed cumin seeds and the remaining salt and pepper and place the tray in the centre of the oven. At the same time, use tongs to turn the sweet potato ribbons over, then return them to the oven.

4. Bake for a further 10 minutes, or until the salmon is cooked through and the potato ribbons are tender and turning golden. If the potatoes need another 1–2 minutes, remove the salmon from the oven and leave to stand while the potatoes finish cooking.

5. Serve the salmon with the potato ribbons and the dressed cucumber ribbons on the side. Garnish with the chopped dill.

MONKFISH, MUSHROOM & RED PEPPER SKEWERS

SERVES: *4* | **PREP:** *15 mins* | **COOK:** *20 mins*

INGREDIENTS

1 tsp salt

160 g/5¾ oz brown basmati rice

400 g/14 oz small chestnut mushrooms, stalks removed

650 g/1 lb 7 oz monkfish tail fillet

1 large red pepper, deseeded

3 back bacon rashers

1½ tbsp olive oil

5 pieces sun-dried tomato, finely chopped

1 tbsp lemon juice

1 large tomato, peeled and finely chopped

1 heaped tsp paprika

1 garlic clove, crushed

fresh coriander sprigs, to garnish

1. Add the salt to a saucepan of water, add the rice, then cover and cook over a low heat for 20 minutes, or until tender but still firm to the bite.

2. Meanwhile, cut any large mushrooms in half. Cut the monkfish tail fillet into 2.5-cm/1-inch cubes and cut the red pepper and bacon into 2.5-cm/1-inch squares. Alternately thread the fish, mushrooms, red pepper and bacon evenly onto four metal skewers.

3. Preheat the grill and brush the kebabs with the oil. Place the kebabs on a rack under the preheated grill and cook for about 4 minutes on each side, or until the fish and bacon are cooked through and the vegetables are tender.

4. To make the sauce, combine the sun-dried tomatoes, lemon juice, tomato, paprika and garlic in a small bowl.

5. Drain the rice. Serve the kebabs with the rice and a spoonful of the sauce. Garnish with coriander sprigs.

SEARED SCALLOPS WITH LIME & CHILLI SAUCE

SERVES: 2 | **PREP:** 5 mins | **COOK:** 45 mins

INGREDIENTS

70 g/2½ oz wild rice

3 tbsp chopped fresh mixed herbs,
  such as parsley, tarragon,
  chives or dill

¼ tsp salt

½ tsp pepper

100 g/3½ oz peas

4 asparagus spears, woody ends
  removed

2 tsp butter

1 tbsp light olive oil

350 g/12 oz large ready-prepared
  scallops, thoroughly dried

3 garlic cloves, crushed

1 small red chilli, deseeded and
  finely chopped

juice and zest of ½ lime

2 tsp sweet chilli dipping sauce

fresh pea shoots, to garnish

1. Rinse the rice under cold running water and drain. Bring a large saucepan of water to the boil, then add the rice. Cook for 40 minutes or until tender, then drain thoroughly. Tip into a serving bowl and leave to cool a little. Stir in the herbs, salt and pepper.

2. Steam the peas and asparagus, with the tips of the asparagus facing upwards, for about 3–4 minutes, or until tender. Cut off the asparagus tips, set aside and keep warm. Chop the asparagus stalks and place them in a blender or food processor with the peas and the butter. Blend until smooth.

3. Brush a frying pan with a little of the oil and place over a high heat. When the pan is really hot, add the scallops. Sear for 1 minute on each side, or until golden and still soft in the centre – don't overcook or the scallops will become dry and chewy. Set aside to keep warm.

4. Reduce the heat to medium. Add the remaining oil with the garlic and chilli and stir-fry for 1 minute, or until soft. Add the lime zest and juice, then add the sweet chilli sauce and stir. Serve the scallops drizzled with the chilli sauce, with the asparagus purée, asparagus tips and rice alongside. Garnish the scallops with fresh pea shoots and serve immediately.

GINGER & SESAME TROUT WITH BRAISED PAK CHOI

SERVES: *2* | **PREP:** *10 mins* | **COOK:** *10 mins*

INGREDIENTS

2 heads of pak choi

½ tbsp groundnut oil

½ tsp Chinese five spice

2 tbsp rice wine

4 tbsp boiling water

1 small green chilli, deseeded and
  finely chopped

6 sprays cooking oil spray

4 rainbow trout fillets

1 tbsp sesame oil

2-cm/¾-inch piece fresh ginger,
  finely grated

1 tbsp low-salt soy sauce

½ tbsp rice vinegar

1 tsp sesame seeds

1 tbsp ketjap manis (Indonesian
  soy sauce)

4 spring onions, chopped, to garnish

1. Quarter each head of pak choi lengthways. Place a large saucepan over a medium–high heat and add the groundnut oil. Add the pak choi and fry for 3 minutes, or until starting to colour. Stir in the five spice and rice wine and cook for a further 1 minute, then add the boiling water and scatter in the chopped chilli. Bring to a simmer, cover, reduce the heat to low and cook for 2–3 minutes, or until the pak choi is just tender.

2. Meanwhile, place a large frying pan over a medium–high heat and spray with 3 sprays of cooking oil spray. Add the trout fillets and cook for 2–3 minutes, then turn over with a spatula. Spray the pan with 3 sprays of cooking spray and cook for a further 2 minutes, or until the fillets are just cooked through. Remove from the pan and keep warm.

3. Reduce the heat to medium, add the sesame oil to the pan and stir in the ginger. Cook for 1 minute, then add the soy sauce, vinegar, sesame seeds and ketjap manis and stir. Serve the trout fillets with the sesame mixture spooned over the top. Garnish with the spring onions and serve with the pak choi on the side.

POACHED SALMON WITH BRAISED BLACK LENTILS

SERVES: *2* | **PREP:** *15 mins* | **COOK:** *40 mins*

INGREDIENTS

1 tbsp extra virgin rapeseed oil

2 shallots, finely chopped

2 garlic cloves, crushed

100 g/3½ oz black (Beluga) lentils

250 ml/9 fl oz vegetable stock

70 g/2½ oz baby spinach

¼ tsp nutmeg

juice of ¼ lemon

2 wild salmon fillets, each weighing
*   125 g/4½ oz*

1 tsp roughly crushed black
*   peppercorns, to garnish*

1. Place a small, lidded frying pan over a medium–low heat and add the oil. Add the shallots and fry, stirring occasionally, for 5 minutes, or until soft and transparent. Add the garlic and stir for 1 minute, then stir in the lentils until coated thoroughly with the oil.

2. Add the stock to the pan, stir and bring to a simmer. Cover and cook for 20 minutes, or until the lentils are tender and most of the stock has been absorbed.

3. Stir in the spinach, nutmeg and lemon juice and cook for a further 2–3 minutes, or until the spinach wilts.

4. Meanwhile, put the salmon fillets in a shallow saucepan, cover with water and bring to a simmer. Cook for 3 minutes, or until just cooked with a hint of pink still in the centre. Drain and cut each fillet into two pieces.

5. Serve the lentils with the salmon pieces on top. Garnish with the black peppercorns and serve immediately.

CHICKEN ESCALOPES WITH CHERRY TOMATOES

SERVES: *4* | **PREP:** *15 mins* | **COOK:** *25 mins*

INGREDIENTS

3 skinless, boneless chicken breasts,
   weighing about 500 g/1 lb 2 oz
   in total

1 egg, beaten

100 g/3½ oz wholemeal panko
   breadcrumbs

1 tsp dried thyme

1 tsp dried oregano

2 tbsp groundnut oil

400 g/14 oz cherry tomatoes on
   the vine

200 g/7 oz baby leaf salad

1 tbsp balsamic vinegar

1. Diagonally slice each chicken breast in four lengthways to make 12 escalopes. Place each escalope on a chopping board and pound it a few times with a rolling pin to a thickness of about 1 cm/½ inch.

2. Put the beaten egg in a shallow dish and put the breadcrumbs in a separate shallow dish. Stir the thyme and oregano into the breadcrumbs until combined.

3. Coat each escalope in egg, allowing the excess to drip off. Dip into the breadcrumb mixture, turning to coat, then transfer to a large plate.

4. Heat the oil in a large, non-stick frying pan. Add the escalopes, in batches, and cook over a medium heat for 4 minutes on each side, or until the breadcrumbs are golden and the escalopes are cooked through, with no sign of pink when you cut into the middle of one of them.

5. Meanwhile, preheat the grill and grill the tomatoes on the vine until warmed through but not collapsed.

6. Serve the escalopes with the grilled tomatoes and the baby leaf salad, drizzled with the balsamic vinegar.

CREOLE CHICKEN WITH CORIANDER PARSNIP RICE

SERVES: *4* | **PREP:** *15 mins* | **COOK:** *30 mins*

INGREDIENTS

2 tbsp extra virgin rapeseed oil

4 small chicken breast fillets, each sliced into 3 equal pieces

1 large onion, sliced

2 celery sticks, finely chopped

1 green pepper, deseeded and thinly sliced

1 yellow pepper, deseeded and thinly sliced

2 garlic cloves, crushed

1 tsp smoked paprika

300 g/10½ oz canned chopped tomatoes

1 tsp sea salt

1 tsp pepper

2 large parsnips, roughly chopped

1 tbsp raw hemp seeds

4 tbsp fresh coriander leaves

fresh coriander sprig, to garnish

1. Heat half the oil in a large frying pan over a high heat. Add the sliced chicken pieces and fry for 2 minutes, or until very lightly browned. Remove the chicken pieces from the pan with a slotted spatula and transfer to a plate. Set aside.

2. Add the onion, celery and green and yellow peppers to the pan with half the remaining oil. Reduce the heat to medium and fry, stirring frequently, for about 10 minutes, or until the vegetables are soft and just turning golden.

3. Stir in the garlic and paprika and cook for 30 seconds. Add the chopped tomatoes and half the salt and pepper. Return the chicken to the pan, bring to a simmer and cook for 10 minutes.

4. Meanwhile, add the parsnips to the bowl of a food processor. Process on high until they resemble rice grains, then stir in the hemp seeds and the remaining salt and pepper.

5. Heat the remaining oil in a frying pan over a medium heat. Stir in the parsnip rice and stir-fry for 2 minutes, then stir through the coriander leaves. Serve the chicken mixture spooned over the parsnip rice, garnished with the coriander sprig.

JERK CHICKEN WITH PAPAYA & AVOCADO SALSA

SERVES: *4* | **PREP:** *35 mins* | **COOK:** *30–35 mins*

INGREDIENTS

1 tsp allspice berries, crushed

1 tsp coriander seeds, crushed

1 tsp mild paprika

¼ tsp freshly grated nutmeg

1 tbsp fresh thyme leaves

1 tbsp black peppercorns, coarsely
    crushed

pinch of salt

1 kg/2 lb 4 oz small chicken
    drumsticks, skinned

1 tbsp olive oil

SALSA

1 papaya, halved, deseeded, peeled
    and cut into cubes

2 large avocados, stoned, peeled
    and cut into cubes

finely grated zest and juice of 1 lime

½ red chilli, deseeded and finely
    chopped

½ red onion, finely chopped

15 g/½ oz fresh coriander, finely
    chopped

2 tsp chia seeds

1. Preheat the oven to 200°C/400°F/Gas Mark 6. Mix the allspice
berries, coriander seeds, paprika, nutmeg, thyme leaves, peppercorns
and salt together in a small bowl.

2. Slash each chicken drumstick two or three times with a knife, then
put them in a roasting tin and drizzle with the oil. Sprinkle the spice
mix over the chicken, then rub it in with your fingers, washing your
hands afterwards.

3. Roast the chicken in the preheated oven for 30–35 minutes, or
until browned, and the chicken is tender and the juices run clear
when a sharp knife is inserted into the thickest part of a drumstick.

4. Meanwhile, to make the salsa, put the papaya and avocados
in a bowl, sprinkle over the lime zest and juice, then toss well.
Add the chilli, red onion, coriander and chia seeds and stir. Serve
immediately.

BAKED CHICKEN WITH
PEARS & HAZELNUTS

SERVES: *4* | **PREP:** *15 mins* | **COOK:** *30 mins*

INGREDIENTS

4 skinless chicken breast fillets,
each weighing about 140 g/5 oz
1½ tbsp extra virgin rapeseed oil
4 large shallots, cut into quarters
2 small pears, peeled, cored and
quartered
100 ml/3½ fl oz dry white wine
2 tsp dried oregano
2 tsp garlic purée
100 ml/3½ fl oz chicken stock
½ tsp salt
½ tsp pepper
40 g/1½ oz blanched hazelnuts,
finely chopped
2 tbsp wholemeal breadcrumbs
2 tbsp chopped fresh parsley
2 tsp fresh thyme leaves

1. Preheat the oven to 180°C/350°F/Gas Mark 4. Cut each of the chicken breasts into two thick steaks. Place a large frying pan over a medium heat and add 1 tablespoon of the oil. Add the shallot quarters and fry for 5 minutes, or until soft and light golden. Set aside until required.

2. Add the chicken and pears to the pan and fry over a high heat for 2–3 minutes, turning once, until light golden (you may need to do this in two batches). Arrange the chicken in a large shallow baking dish, tucking the shallots and pears around the edge.

3. Add the wine to the pan and bring to the boil. Stir in the oregano, half the garlic, all the stock and the salt and pepper. Pour the contents of the pan over the chicken mixture. Bake in the preheated oven for 15 minutes, basting the tops of the chicken pieces with the cooking juices.

4. Meanwhile, combine the hazelnuts, breadcrumbs, parsley and thyme with the remaining oil and garlic in a small bowl. Sprinkle the mixture over the top of the chicken and return to the oven for 10 minutes, or until the top has crisped a little and is lightly golden, and the chicken is tender and the juices run clear when a skewer is inserted into the thickest part of the meat. Serve immediately.

SPICED TURKEY STEW WITH WHOLEGRAIN COUSCOUS

SERVES: *4* | PREP: *20 mins* | COOK: *25 mins*

INGREDIENTS

1 tbsp virgin olive oil
500 g/1 lb 2 oz skinless and
  boneless turkey breast, cut into
  2-cm/¾-inch pieces
1 onion, roughly chopped
2 garlic cloves, finely chopped
1 red pepper, deseeded and roughly
  chopped
1 orange pepper, deseeded and
  roughly chopped
500 g/1 lb 2 oz tomatoes, roughly
  chopped
1 tsp cumin seeds, roughly crushed
1 tsp paprika
finely grated zest and juice of
  1 unwaxed lemon
salt and pepper (optional)

TO SERVE

200 g/7 oz wholegrain giant
  couscous
2 tbsp roughly chopped fresh flat-
  leaf parsley
2 tbsp roughly chopped fresh
  coriander

1. Heat the oil in a large frying pan over a medium heat. Add the turkey, a few pieces at a time, then add the onion. Fry, stirring, for 5 minutes, or until the turkey is golden.

2. Add the garlic, red and orange peppers and tomatoes, then stir in the cumin seeds and paprika. Add the lemon juice and season with salt and pepper, if using. Stir well, then cover and cook, stirring occasionally, for 20 minutes, or until the tomatoes have formed a thick sauce and the turkey is cooked through and the juices run clear with no sign of pink when a piece is cut in half.

3. Meanwhile, half-fill a saucepan with water and bring to the boil. Add the couscous and cook according to the packet instructions, or until just tender. Tip into a sieve and drain well.

4. Spoon the couscous onto plates and top with the turkey stew. Mix the parsley and coriander with the lemon zest, then sprinkle over the stew and serve.

HEALTHY SPAGHETTI
BOLOGNESE

NGREDIENTS

tbsp rapeseed oil

large onion, finely chopped

celery sticks, finely chopped

garlic cloves, crushed

large carrot, finely chopped

00 g/1 lb 2 oz fresh turkey mince

00 g/14 oz canned chopped
  tomatoes

25 g/4½ oz chestnut mushrooms,
  finely chopped

tbsp tomato purée

00 ml/7 fl oz fat-free turkey gravy

tsp instant gravy granules

tsp Italian seasoning

-2 tsp salt

00 g/10½ oz dried wholegrain
  spelt spaghetti

tbsp freshly grated Parmesan
  cheese

1. Place a large, lidded frying pan over a medium–low heat and add the oil. Add the onion and celery and fry, covered, stirring occasionally, for 10 minutes, or until soft and transparent. Stir in the garlic and carrot and cook for a further 1 minute. Push all of the vegetables to the edge of the pan and add the mince to the centre. Increase the heat to medium–high and cook, stirring occasionally, for 2–3 minutes, or until the mince is brown all over.

2. Stir in the tomatoes, mushrooms, tomato purée, gravy, gravy granules and Italian seasoning. Bring to a simmer, reduce the heat to low, cover and cook as gently as you can for 30 minutes, stirring occasionally. Check that all the vegetables are cooked before serving.

3. Meanwhile, add 1–2 teaspoons of salt to a large saucepan of water and bring to the boil. Add the spaghetti and cook for 10 minutes, or until tender but still firm to the bite. Drain the spaghetti and serve in warmed bowls with the sauce spooned over the top, sprinkled with the Parmesan cheese.

BLACK RICE RISOTTO
WITH PARMA HAM

SERVES: *4* | **PREP:** *15 mins* | **COOK:** *1 hour 10 mins*

INGREDIENTS

1 tsp sea salt

200 g/7 oz black rice

6 Parma ham slices

1 tbsp olive oil

*2 small heads of chicory, quartered
    lengthways*

15 g/½ oz butter

2 garlic cloves, thinly sliced

1 small shallot, roughly chopped

500 ml/18 fl oz chicken stock

2 tbsp mascarpone cheese

*2 tbsp roughly chopped fresh flat-
    leaf parsley*

1. Add the salt to a large saucepan of water, bring to the boil, then add the rice and cook for 45 minutes, or until tender but still firm to the bite. Drain and set aside until needed.

2. Heat a deep frying pan over a medium–high heat. Add the ham and fry for 30 seconds on each side, or until crisp. Transfer to a plate

3. Add the oil to the pan, then add the chicory and fry for 2 minutes on each side, or until dark gold in colour. Remove from the pan, wrap in foil to keep warm and set aside.

4. Reduce the heat to medium, then melt the butter in the pan. Add the garlic and shallot and fry for 4 minutes, or until soft. Add the rice and stock, bring to a simmer, then cook gently for 5 minutes, or until two thirds of the liquid has been absorbed. Stir in the mascarpone cheese and parsley, then return the chicory to the pan and heat until warmed through.

5. Crumble the ham into large shards. Heap the risotto into four bowls and serve with the crisp ham on top.

PORK MEDALLIONS WITH POMEGRANATE

SERVES: *4* | **PREP:** *20 mins* | **COOK:** *40–45 mins*

INGREDIENTS

50 g/5½ oz wheatberries
5 g/1 oz fresh flat-leaf parsley,
   roughly chopped
5 g/2 oz kale, shredded
seeds of 1 pomegranate
00 g/1 lb 2 oz pork medallions
tbsp olive oil
garlic cloves, finely chopped

DRESSING

0 g/1¾ oz walnuts,
   roughly chopped
tbsp virgin olive oil
tsp pomegranate molasses
ice of 1 lemon

1. Bring a medium-sized saucepan of water to the boil. Add the wheatberries and simmer for 25–30 minutes, or until tender. Drain and rinse.

2. Meanwhile, to make the dressing, put the walnuts in a large frying pan and toast for 2–3 minutes, or until just beginning to brown. Put the virgin olive oil, molasses and lemon juice in a small bowl and mix together with a fork. Stir in the hot walnuts.

3. Mix the parsley, kale and pomegranate seeds together in a bowl.

4. Remove the visible fat from the pork. Heat the olive oil in the frying pan over a medium heat. Add the pork and garlic and fry for 10 minutes, turning halfway through, until brown and cooked. Cut into the centre of one of the pork medallions – any juices that run out should be clear and piping hot with steam rising. Slice the pork into strips.

5. Add the wheatberries to the kale mixture and gently toss. Transfer to a platter, pour over the dressing, then top with the pork and serve.

LAMB & SPINACH MEATBALLS

SERVES: *4* | **PREP:** *25–30 mins* | **COOK:** *1 hour*

INGREDIENTS

500 g/1 lb 2 oz lean lamb mince

25 g/1 oz fresh breadcrumbs

70 g/2½ oz frozen chopped spinach, thawed

1 tbsp dried oregano

1 tsp ground cumin

1 tbsp olive oil, for frying

TOMATO SAUCE

4 shallots, finely chopped

4 garlic cloves, sliced

25 g/1 oz fresh basil, roughly chopped

1 tbsp tomato purée

800 g/1 lb 12 oz tomatoes, cored and roughly chopped

150 ml/5 fl oz vegetable stock

2 tbsp red wine vinegar

400 g/14 oz wholewheat spaghetti

salt and pepper (optional)

1 tbsp chopped fresh basil, to garnish

1. To make the meatballs, place the mince, breadcrumbs, spinach, oregano and cumin in a large bowl. Gently mix together with damp hands and divide the mixture into 12 portions. Shape each portion into a round meatball.

2. Heat the oil in a deep frying pan over a medium–high heat. Add the meatballs in batches and fry for a few minutes, turning regularly, until brown all over. Remove from the pan and set aside.

3. To make the sauce, add the shallots and garlic to the pan and fry in the residual oil. Add a little more oil if needed and fry until the mixture is soft and beginning to caramelize. Reduce the heat to medium, stir in the basil and tomato purée and cook for a further minute. Stir in the chopped tomatoes and cook for 5–6 minutes, stirring until the tomatoes begin to break down.

4. Add the stock and red wine vinegar and simmer, uncovered, for 25 minutes, or until the sauce has broken down and started to thicken. Return the meatballs to the pan, cover and cook for 12–15 minutes. Season with salt and pepper, if using.

5. Meanwhile, bring a large saucepan of water to the boil, add the spaghetti, bring back to the boil and cook for 12–14 minutes, or until tender but still firm to the bite. Drain, then divide between four bowls. Serve the meatballs and sauce over the spaghetti, garnished with fresh basil.

SPICY STEAK WITH ROASTED SQUASH

SERVES: *4* | **PREP:** *20–30 mins* | **COOK:** *35–40 mins*

INGREDIENTS

*750 g/1 lb 10 oz butternut squash,
  cut into chunks*
4 garlic cloves, finely chopped
*4 large portobello mushrooms, cut
  into thick slices*
*15 g/½ oz finely chopped fresh sage,
  leaves only*
4 tbsp olive oil
4 x 175-g/6-oz fillet steaks
salt and pepper (optional)

CHIMICHURRI SAUCE

25 g/1 oz fresh flat-leaf parsley
½ tsp dried oregano
2 garlic cloves
1 shallot, chopped
¼ tsp dried chilli flakes
grated zest and juice of ½ lemon
2 tbsp red wine vinegar
2 tbsp olive oil
2 tbsp cold water

1. Preheat the oven to 200°C/400°F/Gas Mark 6. Place the squash, garlic, mushrooms and sage in a large roasting tin. Drizzle over 2 tablespoons of the oil and mix well. Season with salt and pepper, if using, and roast in the preheated oven for 25–30 minutes, turning once halfway through the cooking time.

2. Meanwhile, make the sauce. Place all of the ingredients, except the water, in a bowl and blend with a hand-held blender. Carefully pour in the water, adding just enough to reach a spooning consistency. Set aside until needed.

3. Brush the steaks with 1 tablespoon of the oil and season with salt and pepper, if using. Place a heavy frying pan or griddle over a high heat and, once smoking, add the steaks and reduce the heat to medium–high. Cook for 2–3 minutes on each side for medium–rare, or cook to your taste. Remove the steaks from the pan and leave them to rest for a few minutes before serving.

4. Cut the steaks into thick slices and serve on top of the roasted vegetables. Drizzle over the chimichurri sauce and the remaining oil.

LEAN BEEFSTEAKS WITH SPICY BEAN CAKES

SERVES: *2* | **PREP:** *15 mins* | **COOK:** *15 mins*

INGREDIENTS

*1 small sweet potato, weighing
    about 100 g/3½ oz*

½ tbsp olive oil

1 small red onion, finely chopped

2 garlic cloves, crushed

*1 green chilli, deseeded and finely
    chopped*

*200 g/7 oz canned mixed beans,
    drained and rinsed*

2 tbsp fresh breadcrumbs

1 egg yolk

¼ tsp cayenne pepper

1 tsp pepper

½ tsp salt

*2 sirloin steaks, fat band removed,
    each weighing about 150 g/5½ oz*

6 sprays cooking oil spray

1. Prick the skin of the sweet potato with a fork and cook in the microwave on High for 5 minutes, or until just tender. Leave to cool for a few minutes. Meanwhile, place a frying pan over a medium heat and add the oil. Add the onion and fry for 8 minutes, or until soft. Add the garlic and chilli to the pan and fry for a further minute.

2. Mash the beans in a bowl until you have a smooth consistency with a few lumps. Use a slotted spatula to remove the onion mixture from the pan and stir into the beans. Halve the sweet potato, scoop out the flesh and add to the bean mixture with the breadcrumbs, egg yolk, cayenne pepper, pepper and salt. Mix well to combine and shape into four flat round cakes.

3. Reheat the pan, which should still have a thin layer of oil coating it over a medium heat. Add the bean cakes and cook for approximately 3 minutes on each side, or until nicely golden. Meanwhile, place a ridged griddle pan over a high heat. Spray the steaks with the cooking oil spray and, when the pan is very hot, add the steaks and cook for 1½ minutes on each side for rare, or to your liking. Leave to rest for a few minutes, then serve with the bean cakes and any juices that have come from the steaks.

CHAPTER FIVE

BAKING & DESSERTS

PINEAPPLE POWER CHEESECAKE BOWL

SERVES: *4* | **PREP:** *15 mins, plus chilling* | **COOK:** *2 mins*

INGREDIENTS

200 g/7 oz tofu
200 g/7 oz cream cheese
2 tbsp maple syrup
grated rind of 1 orange
2 tbsp pecan nuts
400 g/14 oz fresh pineapple, peeled,
  cored and chopped
2 tbsp desiccated coconut
2 tsp clear honey
8 sweet oat cakes

1. Place the tofu, cream cheese and maple syrup in a food processor and process until smooth.

2. Stir in the orange zest and divide the mixture between four small bowls. Chill in the refrigerator for 10 minutes.

3. Dry-fry the pecan nuts in a small frying pan, then coarsely chop.

4. Divide the pineapple between the bowls, then sprinkle with the chopped nuts and coconut.

5. Drizzle each bowl with a little honey.

6. Serve each portion with two sweet oat cakes.

CHOCOLATE & CHIA PUDDINGS

SERVES: *3* | **PREP:** *20 mins, plus chilling* | **COOK:** *No cooking*

INGREDIENTS

2 tbsp cocoa powder

2 tbsp agave syrup

90 ml/3 fl oz coconut milk

*125 g/4½ oz Greek-style natural
    yogurt*

2 tbsp chia seeds

1 tsp vanilla extract

1 kiwi, sliced, to decorate

*50 g/1¾ oz plain chocolate, roughly
    chopped, to decorate*

1. Place the cocoa powder and agave syrup in a large bowl and mix well to remove any lumps. Stir in the coconut milk, yogurt, chia seeds and vanilla extract and mix thoroughly.

2. Cover and chill in the refrigerator for 4–6 hours. Remove from the refrigerator; the mixture should be quite thick at this stage. Using a hand-held blender, whizz the mixture until smooth and divide between three small dessert glasses.

3. Chill the puddings for a further hour. Decorate with the kiwi slices and chocolate and serve.

COCONUT RICE PUDDING
WITH POMEGRANATE

SERVES: *4* | **PREP:** *15 mins, plus chilling* | **COOK:** *45–50 mins*

INGREDIENTS

55 g/2 oz pudding rice

200 ml/7 fl oz canned light coconut milk

200 ml/7 fl oz almond milk

25 g/1 oz golden caster sugar

1 cinnamon stick

2 gelatine leaves

seeds of 1 pomegranate

¼ tsp grated nutmeg, to sprinkle

1. Place the rice, coconut milk, almond milk, sugar and cinnamon in a saucepan over a high heat. Bring almost to the boil, stirring, then reduce the heat and cover. Simmer very gently, stirring occasionally, for 40–45 minutes, or until most of the liquid is absorbed.

2. Meanwhile, place the gelatine leaves in a bowl and cover with cold water. Leave to soak for 10 minutes to soften. Drain the leaves, squeezing out any excess moisture, then add to the hot rice mixture and lightly stir until the gelatine has completely dissolved.

3. Spoon the rice mixture into four 150-ml/5-fl oz metal pudding basins, spreading evenly. Leave to cool, then cover and chill in the refrigerator until firm.

4. Run a small knife around the edge of each basin. Dip the bases briefly into a bowl of hot water, then turn out onto four plates.

5. Scatter the pomegranate seeds over the rice, then sprinkle with grated nutmeg. Serve immediately.

RASPBERRY &
WATERMELON SORBET

SERVES: *4* | **PREP:** *30 mins, plus cooling & freezing* | **COOK:** *10 mins*

INGREDIENTS

115 g/4 oz golden caster sugar

150 ml/5 fl oz cold water

finely grated zest and juice of 1 lime

225 g/8 oz raspberries

*small watermelon, deseeded,
peeled and cut into chunks*

egg white

1. Put the sugar, water and lime zest in a small saucepan and cook over a low heat, stirring, until the sugar has dissolved. Increase the heat to high, bring to the boil, then reduce the heat to medium and simmer for 3–4 minutes. Remove from the heat and leave to cool.

2. Put the raspberries and watermelon in a food processor in batches and process to a purée, then press through a sieve into a bowl to remove any remaining seeds.

3. Tip the purée into a loaf tin, pour in the lime syrup through a sieve, then stir in the lime juice. Freeze for 3–4 hours, or until the sorbet is beginning to freeze around the edges and the centre is still mushy.

4. Transfer the sorbet to a food processor and process to break up the ice crystals. Put the egg white in a small bowl and lightly whisk with a fork until frothy, then mix it into the sorbet.

5. Pour the sorbet into a plastic or metal container, then cover and freeze for 3–4 hours, or until firm. Remove from the freezer 10 minutes before serving and leave to soften at room temperature.

MIXED FRUIT
SOUP BOWL

SERVES: *4* | **PREP:** *15 mins, plus chilling* | **COOK:** *No cooking*

INGREDIENTS

2 papaya, peeled, deseeded and
chopped
300 g/10½ oz strawberries, hulled
1 honeydew melon, deseeded,
peeled and chopped
15 g/½ oz fresh mint leaves
1 tbsp stem ginger syrup
1 knob stem ginger
100 g/3½ oz blueberries

1. Reserving 1 tablespoon of the papaya, place the remainder in a food processor with 280 g/10 oz of the strawberries and process to a smooth purée.

2. Pour into a jug and chill in the refrigerator for 10 minutes.

3. Meanwhile, place all but 1 tablespoon of the melon in the food processor with half the mint leaves, the ginger syrup and stem ginger. Process to a smooth purée. Pour into a jug and chill in the refrigerator for 10 minutes.

4. When you are ready to serve, divide each soup between four bowl then use a knife to swirl them together. Drop a couple of ice cubes into each bowl.

5. Dice the reserved fruits and sprinkle over the soup with the blueberries and the remaining mint leaves.

TOFU LEMON CHEESECAKE

SERVES: *10* | **PREP:** *35–40 mins, plus chilling* | **COOK:** *5 mins*

INGREDIENTS

BASE

125 g/4½ oz pecan nuts

175 g/6 oz soft dried dates

85 g/3 oz gingernut biscuits

2 tbsp agave syrup

1 tbsp lemon zest, to decorate

FILLING

350 g/12 oz firm silken tofu

300 g/10½ oz full-fat cream cheese

100 g/3½ oz Greek-style natural
   yogurt

grated zest and juice of 3 lemons

100 g/3½ oz soft light brown sugar

½ tsp vanilla extract

15 g/½ oz powdered gelatine

75 ml/2½ fl oz cold water

1. Line a 20-cm/8-inch round springform cake tin with baking paper.

2. To make the base, place the pecan nuts, dates, biscuits and agave syrup in a food processor and pulse until the mixture comes together. The mixture should be slightly sticky when rolled in your hands. Tip the mixture into the prepared tin and press down to evenly over the base.

3. To make the filling, drain any excess water from the tofu and place in a food processor with the cream cheese, yogurt, lemon zest, lemon juice, sugar and vanilla extract. Blend until silky smooth.

4. Place the powdered gelatine in a small bowl and pour over the cold water. Set the bowl over a saucepan of gently simmering water. Stir the gelatine until it has dissolved into the liquid and, working quickly, pour the liquid gelatine into the filling mixture. Blend the filling again until the gelatine is fully incorporated.

5. Spoon the filling on top of the base and chill in the refrigerator for 6 hours or overnight. Serve in slices, decorated with the lemon zest.

HEALTHY APPLE CRUMBLE

SERVES: *6* | **PREP:** *25 mins* | **COOK:** *40–45 mins*

INGREDIENTS

800 g/1 lb 12 oz cooking apples,
peeled, cored and chopped into
2-cm/¾-inch chunks
¼ tsp ground cloves
¼ tsp ground cinnamon
1 tsp ground ginger
3 tbsp soft light brown sugar

TOPPING

200 g/7 oz rolled oats
½ tsp ground cinnamon
3 tbsp clear honey
3 tbsp coconut oil, at room
temperature
50 g/1¾ oz macadamia nuts,
roughly chopped
2 tbsp demerara sugar

1. Preheat the oven to 180°C/350°F/Gas Mark 4.

2. Place the apple chunks in a large saucepan. Add 2 tablespoons of cold water, the cloves, cinnamon, ginger and brown sugar and place over a medium heat. Stew for about 15 minutes, stirring regularly, or until the apples begin to just lose their shape. Put the apples into a 1.2-litre/2-pint baking dish.

3. To make the topping, place the oats in a medium-sized bowl. Stir in the cinnamon, honey, coconut oil, macadamia nuts and demerara sugar and mix well.

4. Sprinkle the topping mixture over the stewed apple and bake for 25–30 minutes, or until golden. Remove from the oven and leave to cool for a few minutes before serving.

CHIA SEED &
BANANA ICE LOLLIES

SERVES: 6 | **PREP:** *20 mins, plus freezing* | **COOK:** *No cooking*

INGREDIENTS

3 large ripe bananas
3 tbsp Greek-style natural yogurt
2 tsp clear honey
2 tsp chia seeds

YOU WILL ALSO NEED

6 x 50-ml/2-fl oz ice lolly moulds
6 ice lolly sticks

1. Blend the bananas, yogurt and honey in a blender or food processor until thick and smooth. Stir in the chia seeds.

2. Transfer the mixture to a jug and pour the mixture evenly into the six ice lolly moulds.

3. Place a lolly stick in the centre of each mould. Place in the freezer and freeze for 6 hours before serving.

4. To unmould the lollies, dip the frozen moulds into warm water for a few seconds and gently release the lollies while holding the sticks.

BANANA FLATBREAD BITES WITH TAHINI & DATE SYRUP

SERVES: *2* | **PREP:** *15–20 mins* | **COOK:** *5–6 mins*

INGREDIENTS

*4 x 20-cm/8-inch wholemeal
   tortillas*
4 tbsp tahini
3 tbsp date syrup
4 bananas, peeled

1. Preheat a dry frying pan, then add the tortillas, one at a time, and warm for 30 seconds on each side.

2. Arrange the tortillas on a chopping board, thinly spread each with the tahini, then drizzle with the date syrup. Add a whole banana to each tortilla, just a little off centre, then roll up tightly.

3. Cut each tortilla into thick slices, secure the bites with a cocktail stick and arrange on a plate. Serve warm.

SWEET POTATO
BROWNIES

MAKES: *12 brownies* | **PREP:** *30 mins, plus cooling* | **COOK:** *20 mins*

INGREDIENTS

olive oil, for oiling

150 ml/5 fl oz olive oil

175 g/6 oz sweet potatoes, coarsely
  grated

100 g/3½ oz stevia

50 g/1¾ oz cocoa powder

½ tsp baking powder

½ tsp bicarbonate of soda

50 g/1¾ oz ground almonds

2 eggs, beaten

20 g/¾ oz walnuts, roughly chopped

1. Preheat the oven to 180°C/350°F/Gas Mark 4. Lightly oil a shallow 19-cm/7½-inch square cake tin, then line it with a large square of baking paper, snipping into the corners diagonally and pressing the paper into the tin so that the base and sides are lined.

2. Put all the ingredients in a large bowl and stir well. Pour the mixture into the prepared tin. Bake in the preheated oven for 20 minutes, or until well risen and the centre is just set.

3. Leave to cool in the tin for 15 minutes. Lift out of the tin using the baking paper, then carefully remove the paper. Cut into 12 brownies to serve.

GINGER, NUT
& OAT BISCUITS

MAKES: *18 biscuits* | **PREP:** *30 mins, plus chilling* | **COOK:** *15 mins*

INGREDIENTS

175 g/6 oz unsalted butter, softened
  and diced, plus extra for greasing
115 g/4 oz dark muscovado sugar
5-cm/1-inch piece fresh ginger,
  peeled and finely chopped
150 g/5½ oz wholemeal plain flour
85 g/3 oz porridge oats
70 g/2½ oz unblanched hazelnuts,
  roughly chopped
70 g/2½ oz unblanched almonds,
  roughly chopped

1. Place a 30-cm/12-inch sheet of baking paper on a work surface.

2. Cream the butter, sugar and ginger together in a large bowl. Gradually beat in the flour, then the oats and nuts, until a soft dough forms. Spoon the mixture into a 25-cm/10-inch line along the baking paper, then press into a 5-cm/2-inch diameter roll. Wrap in the paper and chill in the refrigerator for 30 minutes, or up to 3 days.

3. Preheat the oven to 180°C/350°F/Gas Mark 4. Grease two baking sheets with butter. Unwrap the biscuit dough and slice off as many biscuits as you require. Arrange on the baking sheets, leaving a little space between each biscuit. Bake for 12–15 minutes, or until cracked and brown at the edges.

4. Leave the biscuits to cool on the sheets for 5 minutes, then transfer to a wire rack and leave to cool completely.

CAULIFLOWER & APRICOT SWIRL CHEESECAKE BARS

MAKES: *16 bars* | **PREP:** *15–20 mins, plus cooling and chilling* | **COOK:** *1¼–1½ hours*

INGREDIENTS

sunflower oil, for oiling
250 g/9 oz ready-to-eat dried
apricots
juice of 1 large orange
500 g/1 lb 2 oz low-fat soft curd
cheese
400 ml/14 fl oz natural yogurt
200 g/7 oz golden caster sugar
1 tbsp vanilla extract
4 eggs, lightly beaten
60 g/2¼ oz plain flour
150 g/5½ oz small cauliflower
florets, very finely chopped

BASE

300 g/10½ oz wholemeal flour
50 g/1¾ oz jumbo rolled oats
finely grated rind of 1 large orange
4 tbsp clear honey
150 g/5½ oz unsalted butter

1. Lightly oil a 30 x 24-cm/12 x 9½-inch roasting tin and line with baking paper. Preheat the oven to 180°/350°F/Gas Mark 4.

2. To make the base, mix the flour and oats together. Put the orange rind, honey and butter into a saucepan over a medium heat and hea until melted. Stir into the dry ingredients. Tip the mixture into the prepared tin and firmly press flat. Make sure the corners and edges are firm. Bake in the preheated oven for 15 minutes until crisp.

3. Meanwhile, put the apricots in a small saucepan with the orange juice and enough water to cover by about 2 cm/¾ inch. Bring to the boil, then simmer gently over a medium heat for 7 minutes, or until soft. Tip into a blender or food processor. Purée until smooth, then push through a sieve into a bowl and set aside until needed.

4. Remove the base from the oven and set aside. Reduce the oven temperature to 160°C/325°F/Gas Mark 3.

5. Put the cheese, yogurt, sugar and vanilla extract into a bowl and beat with a hand-held electric mixer until creamy. Beat in the eggs and flour, then gently stir in the chopped cauliflower. Mix half the apricot purée with the cauliflower mixture and pour over the base. Swirl the remaining purée attractively over the top. Do not over-mix

6. Bake for 1–1¼ hours, or until a skewer inserted in the centre comes out clean. Leave to cool completely in the tin, then chill in th refrigerator for 2–8 hours. Slice into 16 bars and serve.

CARROT CAKE MUFFINS

MAKES: *12 muffins* | **PREP:** *15 mins, plus cooling* | **COOK:** *22 mins*

INGREDIENTS

butter, for greasing
~0 g/3¼ oz wholemeal flour
~0 g/2¼ oz plain flour
~tsp bicarbonate of soda
~½ tsp ground cinnamon
~tsp ground ginger
~tsp salt
~65 g/5¾ oz soft light brown sugar
~25 ml/4 fl oz unsweetened apple
sauce
~tbsp sunflower oil
~tsp vanilla extract
~eggs, at room temperature
~carrots, finely shredded
~5 g/1¼ oz raisins
~5 g/1 oz walnuts, chopped

1. Preheat the oven to 180°C/350°F/Gas Mark 4 and grease a 12-hole muffin tin.

2. Put the wholemeal flour, plain flour, bicarbonate of soda, cinnamon, ginger and salt into a medium-sized bowl and mix well.

3. Put the sugar, apple sauce and oil into a separate bowl and beat until well combined. Add the vanilla extract, then add the eggs, one at a time, beating well after each addition.

4. Add the dry mixture to the wet mixture and beat for 1 minute until just combined. Gently stir in the carrots, raisins and walnuts. Scoop the batter into the prepared tin.

5. Bake in the preheated oven for 20–22 minutes, or until a cocktail stick inserted into the centre of a muffin comes out clean. Leave to cool in the tin for a few minutes, then transfer to a wire rack and leave to cool completely. Serve warm or at room temperature.

CHOCOLATE & MACADAMIA CUPCAKES

MAKES: *12 cupcakes* | **PREP:** *30 mins, plus cooling* | **COOK:** *20 mins*

INGREDIENTS

*85 g/3 oz butter, at room
  temperature*
85 g/3 oz crunchy peanut butter
85 g/3 oz light muscovado sugar
2 eggs, beaten
115 g/4 oz wholemeal flour
1 tsp baking powder
*55 g/2 oz macadamia nuts, roughly
  chopped*
*12 whole macadamia nuts, to
  decorate*

CHOCOLATE FROSTING

*100 g/3½ oz plain chocolate, 70%
  cocoa solids, broken into pieces*
25 g/1 oz butter, diced
25 g/1 oz light muscovado sugar
4 tbsp milk

1. Preheat the oven to 180°C/350°F/Gas Mark 4. Line a 12-hole muffin tin with paper cases.

2. Add the butter, peanut butter and sugar to a large bowl or food processor and beat together until light and fluffy.

3. Gradually beat a little of the beaten eggs into the butter mixture, alternating with a few spoonfuls of the flour, then continue until all the eggs and flour have been added and the mixture is smooth. Beat in the baking powder and chopped nuts.

4. Divide the mixture between the paper cases and bake in the preheated oven for 15 minutes until risen, golden brown and the tops spring back when lightly pressed with a fingertip. Leave to cool in the tin for 10 minutes.

5. To make the frosting, put the chocolate, butter, sugar and milk into a bowl set over a saucepan of gently simmering water and heat, stirring occasionally, for about 5 minutes until smooth.

6. Spoon the frosting over the cakes to cover them completely, then top each with a macadamia nut. Leave to cool in the tin for 30 minutes. Remove from the tin and serve, or store any leftovers in a plastic container in the refrigerator for up to 1 day.

LINSEED BISCOTTI

MAKES: *20–24 pieces* | **PREP:** *10 mins, plus cooling* | **COOK:** *40–45 mins*

INGREDIENTS

2 eggs

100 g/3½ oz caster sugar

200 g/7 oz plain flour, plus extra for
    dusting

25 g/1 oz milled linseeds

20 g/¾ oz whole linseeds

½ tsp bicarbonate of soda

¼ tsp ground cinnamon

25 g/1 oz plain chocolate, chopped

20 g/¾ oz pistachio nuts, chopped

20 g/¾ oz dried cranberries

1. Preheat the oven to 180°C/350°F/Gas Mark 4. Line a baking sheet with greaseproof paper. Whisk together the eggs and sugar until light and fluffy.

2. Sift the flour into a bowl and stir in the milled linseeds, whole linseeds, bicarbonate of soda, cinnamon, chocolate, pistachio nuts and cranberries.

3. Pour the egg mixture into the dry ingredients and mix to a soft dough. Turn out onto a floured surface and shape into a 24-cm/9½-inch sausage.

4. Place the sausage on the prepared baking sheet and press a little to flatten to a height of 3 cm/1¼ inches. Bake in the preheated oven for 30 minutes.

5. Remove from the oven and slide onto a chopping board. Reduce the oven temperature to 160°C/325°F/Gas Mark 3. Cut the loaf into 1-cm/½-inch thick slices and return to the baking sheet, cut side up.

6. Bake for 10–15 minutes until crisp, then transfer to a wire rack and leave to cool completely. The biscotti will keep in a tin for up to 3 weeks.

BANANA, GOJI &
HAZELNUT BREAD

MAKES: *1 loaf* | **PREP:** *20 mins, plus cooling* | **COOK:** *1 hour*

INGREDIENTS

*75 g/3 oz butter, softened, plus extra
  for greasing*
115 g/4 oz light muscovado sugar
eggs
*bananas (500 g/1 lb 2 oz
  unpeeled weight), peeled
  and mashed*
115 g/4 oz plain wholemeal flour
115 g/4 oz plain white flour
tsp baking powder
*55 g/2 oz unblanched hazelnuts,
  roughly chopped*
40 g/1½ oz goji berries
40 g/1½ oz dried banana chips

1. Preheat the oven to 180°C/350°F/Gas Mark 4. Grease a 900-g/2-lb loaf tin and line the base and two long sides with baking paper.

2. Cream the butter and sugar together in a large bowl. Beat in the eggs, one at a time, then beat in the bananas. Put the wholemeal flour, white flour and baking powder into a separate bowl and mix well to combine. Add to the banana mixture and beat until smooth. Add the hazelnuts and goji berries and stir well.

3. Spoon the mixture into the prepared tin, smooth the top flat, then sprinkle with the banana chips. Bake in the preheated oven for 50–60 minutes, or until the loaf is well risen, has cracked slightly and a skewer inserted into the centre comes out clean.

4. Leave to cool in the tin for 5 minutes, then loosen the edges with a round-bladed knife and turn out onto a wire rack. Leave to cool completely, then peel away the paper.

FENNEL & CARAWAY
RYE BREAD

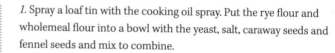

MAKES: *1 loaf* | **PREP:** *30 mins, plus rising* | **COOK:** *30 mins*

INGREDIENTS

5 sprays cooking oil spray
250 g/9 oz dark rye flour
200 g/7 oz strong wholemeal bread
  flour, plus extra for dusting
10 g/¼ oz easy-blend dried yeast
1 tsp salt
1½ tsp caraway seeds, lightly
  crushed
1½ tsp fennel seeds, lightly crushed
2 tsp clear honey
300 ml/10 fl oz lukewarm water
1 tsp caraway seeds, for sprinkling

1. Spray a loaf tin with the cooking oil spray. Put the rye flour and wholemeal flour into a bowl with the yeast, salt, caraway seeds and fennel seeds and mix to combine.

2. Stir the honey into the water and pour into the flour mixture. Mix well until a sticky dough forms.

3. Turn out onto a lightly floured work surface and knead for 5 minutes. Shape the dough into an oblong. Place the dough in the prepared tin, cover with clingfilm and leave in a warm place for 1 hour, or until the dough has doubled in size.

4. Meanwhile, preheat the oven to 220°C/425°F/Gas Mark 7. When the dough has risen, make a few slashes with a sharp knife on the top and sprinkle over the caraway seeds. Bake in the preheated oven for 30 minutes, or until the bread is crisp on the top and the base sounds hollow when tapped. Leave to cool before serving.

APRICOT FLAPJACKS

MAKES: *10 pieces* | **PREP:** *15 mins, plus cooling* | **COOK:** *20–25 mins*

INGREDIENTS

unflower oil, for oiling

75 g/6 oz low-fat spread

5 g/3 oz demerara sugar

5 g/2 oz clear honey

40 g/5 oz dried apricots, chopped

2 tsp sesame seeds

25 g/8 oz porridge oats

1. Preheat the oven to 180°C/350°F/Gas Mark 4. Very lightly oil a 26 x 17-cm/10½ x 6½-inch shallow baking tin.

2. Put the spread, sugar and honey into a small saucepan over a low heat and heat until the ingredients have melted together – do not boil. When the ingredients are warm and well combined, stir in the apricots, sesame seeds and oats.

3. Spoon the mixture into the prepared tin and lightly level with the back of a spoon. Cook in the preheated oven for 20–25 minutes, or until golden brown. Remove from the oven, cut into 10 bars and leave to cool completely before removing from the tin. Store the flapjacks in an airtight tin and consume within 2–3 days.

HONEYED CARROT
& PECAN SQUARES

MAKES: *15 squares* | **PREP:** *25 mins* | **COOK:** *30 mins*

INGREDIENTS

3 eggs

150 ml/5 fl oz virgin olive oil

115 g/4 oz light muscovado sugar

5 tbsp set honey

175 g/6 oz plain wholemeal flour

4 tbsp wheatgerm

2 tsp baking powder

2 tsp ground ginger

grated zest of 1 orange

1¼ tsp mixed spice

175 g/6 oz carrots, coarsely grated

55 g/2 oz pecan nuts, broken into
*   pieces*

FROSTING

115 g/4 oz Greek-style natural
*   yogurt*

150 g/5½ oz cream cheese or
*   mascarpone cheese*

1. Preheat the oven to 180°C/350°F/Gas Mark 4. Line a 18 x 28-cm/ 7 x 11-inch roasting tin with baking paper, snipping into the corners diagonally and pressing the paper into the tin so that the base and sides are lined.

2. Break the eggs into a large bowl, add the oil, sugar and 4 tablespoons of the honey and whisk until smooth. Put the flour, wheatgerm and baking powder in a small bowl, then add the ginger, most of the orange zest and 1 teaspoon of the mixed spice and stir. Add the dry ingredients to the egg mixture and whisk again until smooth. Add the carrots and most of the pecan nuts and stir.

3. Spoon the mixture into the prepared tin and spread in an even layer. Bake in the preheated oven for 30 minutes, or until well risen and a skewer inserted into the centre comes out clean. Remove the cake from the tin, peel off the baking paper and turn out onto a wire rack. Leave to cool completely.

4. Meanwhile, to make the frosting, put the yogurt, cream cheese and remaining honey and mixed spice into a bowl and beat until smooth. Spread the frosting over the cake, then sprinkle with the remaining pecan nuts and orange zest. Cut into 15 squares and serve.

SUMMER BERRY
SPONGE CAKES

MAKES: *6 cakes* | **PREP:** *25 mins, plus cooling* | **COOK:** *15 mins*

INGREDIENTS

sunflower oil, for oiling
3 eggs
85 g/3 oz golden caster sugar
½ tsp vanilla extract
85 g/3 oz brown rice flour
250 g/9 oz fat-free Greek-style
  natural yogurt
400 g/14 oz mixed raspberries,
  blueberries and sliced
  strawberries
1 tbsp icing sugar, sifted

1. Preheat the oven to 180°C/350°F/Gas Mark 4. Brush 6 x 175-ml/ 6-fl oz ring tins with a little oil and place them on a baking sheet.

2. Put the eggs, caster sugar and vanilla extract in a large bowl and beat with an hand-held electric mixer for 5 minutes, or until the mixture is thick and leaves a trail when the whisk is lifted.

3. Sift the flour over the egg mixture, then gently fold it in with a large metal spoon. Spoon the mixture into the prepared tins and ease into an even layer, being careful not to knock out any air.

4. Bake in the preheated oven for 12–15 minutes, or until the cakes are risen and golden brown and beginning to shrink away from the edges of the tins.

5. Leave to cool in the tins for 5 minutes. Loosen the edges of the cakes with a round-bladed knife, turn them out onto a wire rack and leave to cool completely.

6. Put the cakes on serving plates, spoon the yogurt into the centre, then pile the fruits on top. Dust with sifted icing sugar and serve.

INDEX

···· ✗ ····

This edition published by Parragon Books Ltd in 2017
LOVE FOOD is an imprint of Parragon Books Ltd

Parragon Books Ltd
Chartist House
15–17 Trim Street
Bath BA1 1HA, UK
www.parragon.com/lovefood

ISBN 978-1-4748-6894-5

Printed in China

Edited by Fiona Biggs
Cover photography by Al Richardson

The cover shot shows the Rainbow Rice & Bean Salad on
page 88.

.... Notes for the Reader ....

This book uses both metric and imperial measurements.
Follow the same units of measurement throughout;
do not mix metric and imperial. All spoon measurements
are level: teaspoons are assumed to be 5 ml, and tablespoons
are assumed to be 15 ml. Unless otherwise stated, milk
is assumed to be full fat, eggs and individual fruits and
vegetables are medium, pepper is freshly ground black
pepper and salt is table salt. Unless otherwise stated,
all root vegetables should be peeled prior to using.

The times given are an approximate guide only.
Preparation times differ according to the techniques used
by different people and the cooking times may also vary
from those given.

While the publisher of the book and the original author(s)
of the recipes and other text have made all reasonable
efforts to ensure that the information contained in this
book is accurate and up to date at the time of publication.

Anyone reading this book should note the following
important points: -

Medical and pharmaceutical knowledge is constantly
changing and the author(s) and the publisher cannot and
do not guarantee the accuracy or appropriateness of the
contents of this book;

In any event, this book is not intended to be, and should
not be relied upon, as a substitute for appropriate, tailored
professional advice. Both the author(s) and the publisher
strongly recommend that a doctor or other healthcare
professional is consulted before embarking on major
dietary changes;

For the reasons set out above, and to the fullest extent
permitted by law, the author(s) and publisher: (i) cannot
and do not accept any legal duty of care or responsibility in
relation to the accuracy or appropriateness of the contents
of this book, even where expressed as 'advice' or using
other words to this effect; and (ii) disclaim any liability,
loss, damage or risk that may be claimed or incurred as a
consequence – directly or indirectly – of the use and/or
application of any of the contents of this book.